Exploring the Oceans

Exploring the Oceans

Science Activities for Kids

Anthony D. Fredericks

Illustrated by Shawn Shea

FULCRUM RESOURCES
GOLDEN, COLORADO

To Abigail—
May her world be filled with oceans of discoveries.

Library of Congress Cataloging-in-Publication Data
Fredericks, Anthony D.
    Exploring the oceans : science activities for kids / Anthony D.
Fredericks ; illustrated by Shawn Shea.
        p.   cm.
    Includes bibliographical references and index.
    Summary: Presents information about the oceans of the world, the life they support, their importance as an ecosystem, and the threats they face. Includes related activities.
    ISBN 1-55591-379-2 (pbk.)
    1. Oceanography—Juvenile literature. 2. Oceanography—Study and teaching—Activity programs—Juvenile literature. [1. Ocean. 2. Marine ecology. 3. Ecology.] I. Berlute-Shea, Shawn, ill. II. Title.
GC21.5.F74   1998
551.46—dc21   98-15688
                                              CIP
                                               AC

Printed in the United States of America

0 9 8 7 6 5 4 3 2 1

Fulcrum Publishing
350 Indiana Street, Suite 350
Golden, Colorado 80401-5093
(800) 992-2908 • (303) 277-1623
www.fulcrum-resources.com • fulcrum@fulcrum-resources.com

Contents

Acknowledgments

The author is indebted to the staff at the Oregon Coast Aquarium in Newport, Oregon, for their assistance in providing relevant materials and information during the research for this book. The Oregon Coast Aquarium is a testament to the commitment, dedication, and outreach efforts of marine scientists and educators worldwide who work to preserve this planet's oceans and share their wonders with youngsters everywhere.

Note: The Oregon Coast Aquarium was recently named one of the top ten aquariums in the United States by *Parade* magazine. Be sure to check out their incredible website: http://www.aquarium.org.

Introduction

An ancient ship—more than 300 years old and filled with gold coins, iron muskets, and ceramic vases—lies buried off a Caribbean island. An army of sea snakes more than 10 miles long wriggles across the surface of the crystal blue waters of the South Pacific. A giant squid with an arm span of more than 30 feet, darts from rocky ledge to rocky ledge in search of food in the frigid Arctic Ocean near the coast of Alaska. A school of tuna zooms through the water at speeds of more than 35 mph hunting for prey. A pod of whales surfaces, blows a stream of water vapor from their blowholes, and crashes into the water with both majesty and grace. This is the ocean—a magical and majestic environment that covers nearly two-thirds of the earth's entire surface—an environment that harbors incredible creatures and mysterious events.

The five major oceans of the world contain more life than any other ecosystem of the world. They are home to the world's largest creature of all time—the blue whale—and have some of the planet's smallest creatures—diatoms, plankton, and other one-cell organisms. You'll find a world of extremes in the oceans—the tallest mountains and deepest valleys, the heaviest and lightest fish, and the hottest and coldest waters anywhere on the planet. The longest worm (the bootlace worm grows to be more than 55 yards long), the fastest animal (the sailfish can swim at speeds of more than 68 mph—faster than a cheetah can run), the most poisonous animal (the box jellyfish's venom can kill a human in 30 seconds), the highest producer of eggs (the ocean sunfish produces 300 million eggs a year), and the smallest fish (the Marshall Islands goby is less than half an inch from nose to tail) all inhabit the world's oceans.

The oceans of the world are where new discoveries are being made every day and where new and incredible adventures await those willing to make those discoveries. In fact, many biologists estimate that somewhere between 500,000 and 5,000,000 marine species have yet to be discovered and described. From sea

treasures on sunken pirate ships to vast deposits of precious minerals and amazing new creatures, the undiscovered reaches of the world's oceans are infinite.

But all the oceans are in danger! Humans are dumping their garbage and toxic pollutants into the ocean. Large ocean tankers are discharging millions of gallons of oil into the ocean every year. Fishing fleets from many nations are over-fishing many different species of fish to the point of endangerment or, worse, extinction. Some scientists estimate that many parts of the world's oceans are so endangered that it will take heroic efforts by entire nations to bring them back to a state of normalcy. What we do as citizens in the next few years will have a major impact on the survival of oceans and their inhabitants for generations to come.

The health of many areas of the world's oceans can be described as threatened, critical, or terminal. Just because you may not live near an ocean doesn't mean that oceans aren't a part of your life. The food you eat, the medicines you take, the recreation or vacations you share with your family may all be dependent upon the health of the world's oceans—those that border the United States as well as those that fringe other countries throughout the world. Taking an active role in learning about the world's oceans will provide you with important information that you can use to help preserve and protect these magnificent bodies of water for years to come.

This book is designed to provide you with exciting and fascinating information about the oceans of the world. It contains lots of hands-on activities and projects to help you learn about various aspects of this important ecosystem. You'll learn how to build a miniature ocean right in your own living room; you'll learn how to prepare recipes using different types of foods from the ocean; and you'll build models and conduct a wide variety of ocean experiments that will help you to appreciate oceans as a regular part of your everyday life. I invite you to tackle as many of the projects as you wish. Of course, the more you attempt, the more opportunities you will have to learn about oceans and all their mysteries. Each of the activities, experiments, and projects in this book has been designed to provide you with valuable learning experiences so that you might appreciate and work for the preservation of this important ecosystem.

How to Use This Book

This is a book full of discoveries and full of wonder—a book where you'll finds lots to explore and lots to do. Here you'll get firsthand experiences in learning about and appreciating various elements of the world's oceans. There are projects you can do indoors, discoveries you can make in your own community, and stuff to learn everywhere you go. This book will not only tell you about parts of the oceans, it will show you what an ocean is all about. You won't need a lot of equipment or expensive supplies—there are loads of ocean activities, projects, and discoveries for everyone within the pages of this book.

Throughout this book you'll see several symbols such as those below. These symbols identify an activity, experiment, or project for you to try.

 This symbol stands for an *activity* or *experiment*. The activities in this book are designed to help you appreciate selected portions of the oceans and participate in real hands-on learning experiences.

 This is a *look for it project*—something you can do in your own community, your kitchen at home, or outdoors. These projects will help you compare parts of your local environment with the world's oceans.

It is not necessary to complete every investigation in this book. You should feel free to select those activities that you are most comfortable with or that you find most interesting. I sincerely hope you enjoy your journey through the oceans of the world with their fascinating creatures, wonderful landforms, and incredible mysteries.

Welcome to the Oceans

They're big! They're huge! They're enormous! They cover more than two-thirds of the surface of the earth. They are filled with some of the most amazing, incredible, and fantastic creatures, plants, and geological formations any human being has ever seen.

What are they? They're the oceans of the world. Covering nearly 70 percent of the earth's surface, the oceans contain nearly 97 percent of the planet's entire water supply. In fact, of all the planets in the solar system, ours is the most watery. If you could travel into space (stand on the moon, for example) and look back at the earth you would be able to see why it's sometimes called "The Water Planet"—indeed, the oceans of the world can be easily seen from the far out reaches of the universe.

Let's take a look at the five major oceans of the world and some of their distinguishing features and characteristics:

Pacific Ocean

- This is the largest ocean in the world covering about one-third of the entire planet, or 63,800,000 square miles.
- It reaches almost halfway around the world at its widest point, which is approximately 11,000 miles.
- It's the deepest ocean with an average depth of 13,215 feet.
- The Mariana Trench, off the Philippines, is the deepest part of any ocean and the deepest point on earth. It reaches a depth of 36,200 feet (28 Empire State Buildings, one on top of the other, would easily fit in the trench).
- It covers an area twice the size of the second largest ocean, the Atlantic.
- It contains more than one-half of all the seawater on earth—almost as much as that of the Atlantic and Indian Oceans combined.

- The Pacific has more underwater volcanoes (or seamounts) than any other ocean. It also has the most number of islands.

Atlantic Ocean

- It's the second largest ocean covering an area of about 31,830,000 square miles, or one-fifth of the earth's surface.
- It's widest point is 5,965 miles across.
- It has an average depth of 12,880 feet and is 28,374 feet deep at its deepest point (that's almost as deep as Mt. Everest is tall).
- It contains some of the world's richest fishing grounds. About 90 percent of all fish caught for food comes from the Atlantic.
- The Mid-Atlantic Ridge, which runs north-south for nearly 7,000 miles, is the longest mountain chain in the world.

Indian Ocean

- It's the third largest of the world's oceans covering an area of 28,360,000 square miles.
- It has an average depth of 13,002 feet and its deepest point is at 24,441 feet.
- It contains the saltiest sea (the Red Sea) and the warmest gulf (the Persian Gulf).
- Unlike other oceans, with currents that follow the same path all year long, currents in the this ocean change course twice a year.
- Some of the flattest places in the world can be found in the mid-Indian Ocean basin.

Antarctic Ocean

- It's the fourth largest of the world's oceans covering an area of 13,500,000 square miles.
- In winter, more than half of this ocean is covered with ice and icebergs.
- This ocean includes all the waters south of latitude 55°S.

Arctic Ocean

- It's the smallest and shallowest of the world's oceans covering an area of 5,440,000 square miles.

- It has an average depth of 3,953 feet with a maximum depth of 17,880 feet.
- It is the only ocean almost completely surrounded by land.
- The majority of its waters are covered by sheets of ice, which can be more than 160 feet thick in winter.

Did You Know?

The terms "sea" and "ocean" are often used interchangeably. But an ocean and a sea are not quite the same thing. A *sea* is defined as a body of water that is partly or totally enclosed by land. Here are some examples of seas:

- Arabian Sea
- Bering Sea
- Black Sea
- Caribbean Sea
- Coral Sea
- Mediterranean Sea
- North Sea
- Philippine Sea
- Red Sea
- Sea of Japan
- Tasman Sea
- Weddell Sea

A *gulf* is part of an ocean that dents into the land. Examples of gulfs include:

- Gulf of Alaska
- Gulf of California
- Gulf of Mexico
- Persian Gulf

Saltwater Soup

If you've ever been to the ocean you know that the water is salty. But have you ever thought about how ocean water became salty in the first place? It's actually due to a number of factors, but is basically the result of the earth's water cycle. Salt is one of the primary minerals found in soil over the entire earth's crust. Rain and other forms of precipitation fall on the earth and wash the salt into rivers and streams. The rivers and streams then carry the salt into the ocean where it is mixed with water.

Salt (chemical name: sodium chloride) is dissolved throughout seawater. But, there are other "salts" that can be found in seawater including bicarbonate, potassium, calcium, magnesium, sulfate, sodium, chloride, and traces of other salts.

The saltiness, or *salinity,* of seawater is measured as the parts of salt per 1,000 parts of seawater (ppt). For example, the average salinity of ocean water is 35 ppt. That means that there are 35 pounds of salt per 1,000 pounds of seawater.

3

 Tons of Salt

This activity will help you separate salt from salt water.

You'll need:

large glass jar
water
saucepan
salt
wooden stirring spoon
piece of string
paper clip
pencil

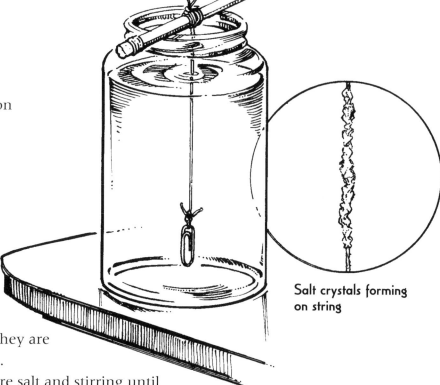

Salt crystals forming on string

What to do:

1. Fill the saucepan about $^3/_4$ full with warm water.
2. Add several table-spoons of salt to the water and stir until they are completely dissolved.
3. Continue adding more salt and stirring until no more salt can dissolve.
4. Put the saucepan on the stove and heat the water until it is hot (not boiling).
5. Remove the saucepan from the stove and stir in 1 or 2 more tablespoons of salt.
6. Allow the solution to cool and pour it into the glass jar.
7. Tie one end of the string to the middle of the pencil and tie the other end to a paper clip (for weight).
8. Place the pencil across the jar's mouth and put the string into the solution in the jar, but don't let the paper clip touch the bottom of the jar. (If necessary wrap it a few more times around the pencil.)
9. Place the jar in a warm undisturbed location for several days.

Alternate method:

Cover the bottom of a cookie sheet with black construction paper. Prepare the saltwater mixture as in the description above (steps 1–5). After the saltwater mixture has cooled, pour the salty water over the paper to a depth of about a $^1/_2$

inch. Place the cookie sheet in a sunny location outside or by a window indoors. Observe the paper until all the water has evaporated.

What happens:

As the water evaporates, the salt that is in solution in the water will adhere to the string (or form on the surface of the construction paper) and return to a solid state. You will be able to remove the string and see the salt crystals forming on it (or you will be able to see white crystals on the paper surface).

Ocean water has a specific level of salinity that varies according to temperature, location, water currents, dissolved minerals, and other factors. The solution you created in this activity is much more salty than any ocean water.

Density

Density measures how heavy something is for its size. For example, if you had a quart of one liquid and a quart of another liquid and they both weighed the same, then you could say that they both had the same density too. However, if one quart of liquid weighed more than a quart of another type of liquid, then the first liquid would have a greater density than the second.

Salt water has greater density than an equivalent amount of fresh water. That's because of all the extra salts and minerals dissolved in seawater. You can prove this to yourself by filling two identical clear plastic cups with equal amounts of fresh water and salt water (four ounces each, for example). Place one cup on the pan at one end of a simple balance scale and the other cup on the pan at the other end. You'll note that the cup with salt water weighs more than the cup with fresh water, even though they both contain the same quantity of liquid. That's because salt water is more dense than fresh water.

Ocean Geography

Many people imagine the ocean to be just deep and flat. In fact, the ocean has as many different shapes and elevations as does the dry land above it. If you could imagine all the water was sucked out of the world's oceans you could see this amazing landscape. Tall mountains, deep valleys, slopes, plains, trenches, and ridges can be found throughout most of the oceans of the world. What you would see is a landscape that is quite similar, and certainly no less dramatic, as that found throughout North America. With modern scientific instruments and exploration ships we have been able to learn a great deal about the geography of the world's oceans.

For a moment, let's imagine we could take a side view of the ocean by cutting through the ocean floor with a very sharp (and very large) knife. Here are the different areas we would discover (please refer to the accompanying illustration):

Continental Shelf

The continental shelf is the edge of the continent that is underwater. The surface of the continental shelf usually slopes gently downward although its width may vary considerably. For example, the continental shelf off the West Coast of the United States is very *narrow,* while on certain sections of the East Coast the shelf may be very *wide* (up to 260 miles wide). The continental shelf is defined as that area from the shoreline out to a distance of about 667 feet.

This part of the ocean has the greatest concentration of plants and animal life. Sunlight can reach the floor in many places and large numbers of fish make their home in this region of the ocean. This is also the area of the ocean where most commercial fishing takes place.

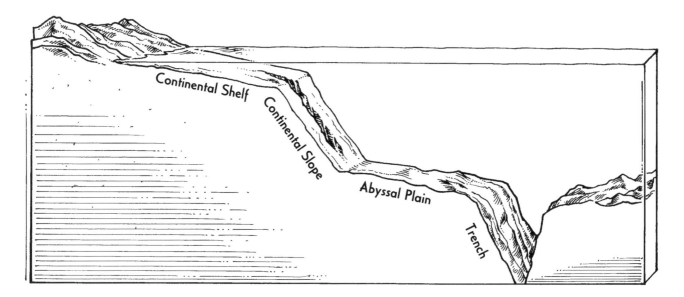

Continental Slope

As we get farther from the continent and the ocean continues to get deeper we reach the area known as the continental slope. This area forms a steep drop from the continental shelf, often consisting of deep canyons. Some of these canyons are considerably deeper than the Grand Canyon.

Abyssal Plains

At the bottom of the continental slope are wide flat areas known as abyssal plains. These plains are very similar to the plains we know on the land surface of the earth. Broad expanses of flat land, occasionally broken up by other types of geological formations, are as characteristic of abyssal plains as they are of the Great

Plains of the United States. The deepest part of this area of the ocean is known as the *abyss*, which has an average depth of approximately 15,000 feet.

Scattered throughout the abyssal plains are other geological formations. These include:

OCEANIC RIDGE

This is a long, continuous mountain range that rises up when a new sea floor wells up from inside the earth. These mountain ranges are connected forming an enormous mountain system that is more than 40,500 miles long. The average height of these mountain ranges is about $1^1/_2$ miles above the ocean floor.

SEAMOUNTS

This is a single underwater mountain that rises up from the ocean floor. Some of them may be more than 4 miles high. Seamounts with flat tops are known as *guyots*. Seamounts that rise above the surface of the ocean are known as *islands*.

BASIN

A basin is a huge, bowl-shaped dent in the ocean floor. It looks like part of the ocean floor has been gently hollowed out—similar to a cereal bowl pressed into the mud.

OCEANIC TRENCH

This is a long narrow valley in the sea floor. Usually found near islands or coastal mountain ranges, it consists of some of the deepest areas of the ocean. The Mariana Trench in the Pacific Ocean is 36,200 feet deep.

OOZE

On the bottom of the ocean floor is a gooey, muddy mixture known as ooze. This layer, which can be as thick as 2,000 feet, consists of dust blown out to sea by winds, particles of dead sea organisms that drift down from the upper levels, volcanic ash from undersea volcanoes, and other types of debris.

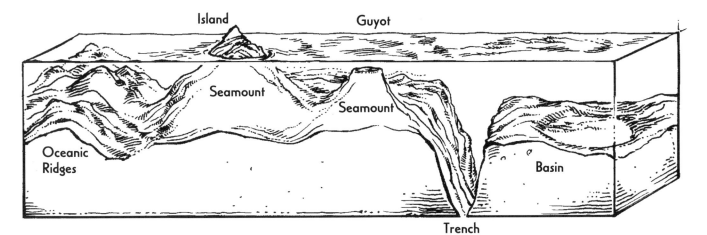

Chains and Webs

All life starts with energy from the sun. Through photosynthesis, this light energy is transformed by plants into chemical energy. This energy is then used to produce food. Because plants can produce their own food, they are known as *producers.*

Plants are eaten by many different varieties of animals. Because animals need to eat plants to survive and because they cannot produce their own food, they are known as *consumers.* There are three different types of consumers: *herbivores* (animals that eat only plants); *carnivores* (animals that eat only animals); and *omnivores* (animals that eat both plants and animals). Human beings are omnivores because our diet is a combination of both plant and animal life.

When plants or animals die, organisms known as *decomposers* (bacteria, algae, fungi, worms, etc.) break down the dead plant or animal tissues and return the nutrients to the environment. The plants and animals in a given environment are thus linked together in a complex series of feeding relationships. Plants produce food. This food is eaten by some animals, providing the energy they need to survive. These animals may then be eaten by other (usually larger) animals. In turn, those animals may be eaten by another group of (even larger) animals. Eventually, those large animals may be killed or may die naturally. They will then decompose and become food for much smaller plants and animals.

This series of stages in which one organism is dependent on another organism for survival (and so on) is known as a *food chain.* For example, look at the following food chain:

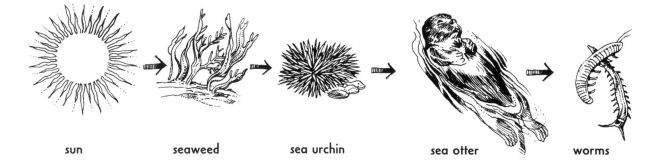

| sun | seaweed | sea urchin | sea otter | worms |

In this illustration, you can see that seaweed (producer) uses energy from the sun to produce its own food. A sea urchin (consumer) eats the seaweed and obtains energy from the seaweed. A sea otter (consumer) locates and eats the sea urchin, obtaining energy from the sea urchin. Eventually the sea otter dies and bacteria and worms (decomposers) attack its body and return its nutrients to the surrounding environment.

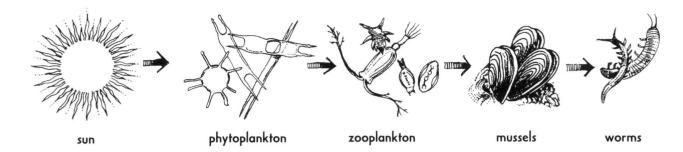

| sun | phytoplankton | zooplankton | mussels | worms |

In this illustration you'll note that *phytoplankton* (microscopic ocean plants) get their energy from the sun. Those plants are then consumed by *zooplankton* (microscopic ocean animals). The zooplankton is then eaten by mussels attached to the pilings of a pier. Later, the mussels die and are decomposed by an army of worms and bacteria.

As you look at food chains, you might expect that the consumption of one organism by another, which in turn is consumed by another organism, might happen in a straight line. However, nature is never quite that simple. Several organisms may be involved at several different levels, each dependent on several others for its food supply (for example, a sea gull may eat clams, oysters, mussels, *and* crabs). This type of arrangement is known as a *food web*. Since most organisms eat more than one type of food, most organisms belong to more than one food chain. When several different chains are combined they form a food web.

 All Tied Together

You'll need:

> index cards
> yarn
> single-hole paper punch
> markers

What to do:

1. Use the diagram on page 10, which illustrates a marine food web.
2. Print the name of each organism in the web on an index card.
3. Lay the index cards out on a large flat surface (table or floor) as in the diagram below.
4. Lay pieces of yarn between the cards to represent the lines in the diagram below.
5. Use the paper punch to punch the necessary holes in each card.
6. Tie the ends of each piece of yarn to each of the punched holes.

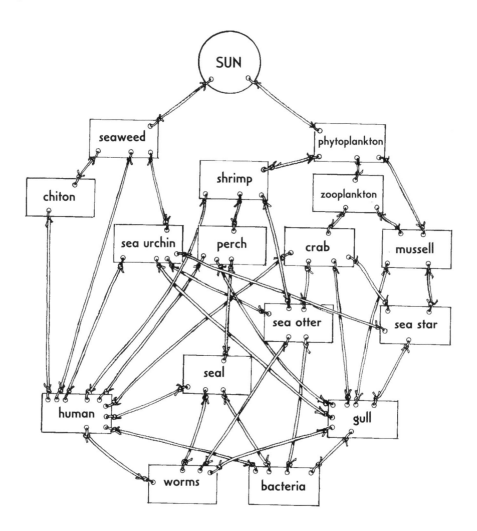

What happens:

You will note that there are a number of food chains represented in the food web you created (for example: sun → phytoplankton → shrimp → perch → gull → bacteria *and* sun → seaweed → sea urchin → sea otter → worms). In short, there is a complex series of relationships that exists in the oceans, relationships that help ensure the survival of the greatest number of plant and animal species possible; every plant and animal in the ocean is dependent on every other plant and animal in the ocean in order to live and survive.

The ocean is a magical, mysterious, and magnificent world full of discoveries and full of amazing features and incredible creatures. Throughout this book you will have many opportunities to learn about this unique ecosystem—how it works, what it contains, and how it contributes to our everyday lives. So put on your wet suit, grab a fishing pole, and get set for a wonderful, delightful, and fantastic voyage!

2 Seashores and Tide Pools

Waves crash, sending spray in a dozen different directions. Clams dig in the mud. Small fish swim through pools of water. Strange sea creatures cling to rocks. Broken shells dot the landscape. Snails and other animals slide over algae-covered boulders. Worms burrow into the sand. Crabs scuttle from one hiding place to another.

This is the seashore—an exciting environment full of life and discoveries. Creatures, both large and small, call this dynamic place their home. Plants, too, survive in this often difficult and frequently spectacular ecosystem. This is a rich and varied community of magic and mysteries—all waiting for you to discover.

Tide Pools

Tide pools are pools of water left behind when the ocean recedes at low tides. These pools may be trapped in the nooks and crannies of rocks, between rock ledges and sand, or in depressions along the beach. Water in these pools is filled with a wide variety of plants and animals—some creatures are *microscopic* (too small to be seen without the aid of a microscope)—while many are considerably larger and can be located quite easily.

The organisms that live in tide pools must be hardy survivors. Waves wash in and out of the pools, moving sand and debris back and forth across both plants and animals. Harsh storms roll in to dump tons of seawater on the pools. Sometimes the pools are exposed to the sun and air, while at other times they may be submerged under water. Tide pool organisms also must be able to locate food necessary for their survival, while, at the same time, avoid becoming a meal for other organisms.

Water, sand, rocks, and debris ebb and flow in and out of tide pools and so do new plants and animals. In fact, you could visit the same tide pool many times and never see the same organisms twice. Tide pools are truly dynamic environments.

Tides

Tides are the natural rise and fall of water along the ocean's shore. Tides are caused by the pull of the moon's gravity on earth as the earth spins around on its axis once every 24 hours. When the moon's gravity pulls seawater toward land, the water level rises—this is high tide. High tide is when much of the shoreline is covered by water. When the moon pulls water away from land, the sea level falls—this is low tide. Low tide is when much of the shoreline is exposed to the air.

Every day the ocean washes up onto the shore until it reaches a certain point (the high tide mark), then it begins to recede until it reaches a low point (the low tide mark). These high and low points occur approximately 6 hours apart. That means that during a 24-hour day there will be two high tides and two low tides.

Many newspapers list the tide times for the day or week. Also, you can often obtain tide books from fishing tackle stores, bait shops, boat landings, marinas, and marine aquariums.

You can also obtain East and West Coast tide tables from the National Ocean Service (NOS) for $10.00 each. Make a check payable to the Department of Commerce—NOS, and mail it to:

NOAA Distribution Branch, N/CG33
National Ocean Service
Riverdale, MD 20737

Intertidal Zone

The intertidal zone is the selected area of the shoreline exposed or covered by the tides. The intertidal zone extends from the highest wave-slashed rocks on top down to areas of the shore that are exposed only by infrequent, extremely low tides. Different plants and animals live up and down the intertidal zone depending on how well they can tolerate exposure to the air and the crashing of the waves, or locate appropriate food sources. Organisms that need to be underwater a lot (fish, seaweed, crabs) live near the bottom of the intertidal zone. Other organisms that can tolerate both wet and dry conditions (barnacles, algae, limpets) live near the top of the intertidal zone.

On both coasts of the United States the intertidal zone is divided into three sections—the high-tide zone, the mid-tide zone, and the low tide zone. You will learn more about the characteristics of these zones, and some organisms that live in each one, in this chapter.

HIGH-TIDE ZONE

This highest zone is characterized by organisms that must endure the harshest extremes of life. Plants and animals that live in this region must be able to endure

bright sunlight, dehydration, and rapid changes in temperature. At high tide they are covered by cold water; at low tide they are high and dry, being exposed to sun and wind.

This portion of the shoreline is underwater (submerged) during high tides and exposed to the air during low tides. During a period of 24 hours this section will be dry for about half of that time and wet for the other half of the time.

Just above the high-tide zone is the "splash zone," which is above the reach of the highest tide. It is wet due to the spray and splash of waves beating below it.

The *dominant* or *indicator* organisms (organisms that always inhabit an area and that can be used to help identify a specific intertidal zone) for the high-tide zone are barnacles and algae.

Selected High-Tide Organisms

Barnacles

What they look like:

Barnacles have shells of connected over-lapping plates. They are $^1/_2$ to 1 inch wide and are volcano-shaped. Depending on the species, they may be white, brown, pink, or black.

Acorn barnacle

Where they live:

They can be found all along the Pacific shoreline from Alaska south to Mexico.
They also inhabit the Atlantic Coast from Canada south to Florida.

How to find them:

They glue themselves to rocks, ships, pilings, and even living creatures such as whales and abalones.
Their habitats vary from exposed shorelines to protected bays.

Fascinating facts:

Most species of barnacles are hermaphroditic—they are both male and female at the same time.
The "glue" that holds a barnacle to rocks is one of the strongest known natural adhesives.

Mole Crabs

What they look like:

Mole crabs are about 1 to $1^1/_2$ inches long. The body, which is shaped like a football or small egg, is gray-pink in color.

The tailpiece of a mole crab is bent forward under the body in order to protect it. This makes the mole crab look like a compressed shrimp.

Mole crab

Where they live:

The Pacific Mole Crab can be found all along the Pacific Coast from Alaska south to Peru and Chile. The Atlantic Mole Crab can be found from Cape Cod to Mexico.

How to find them:

Mole crabs move up and down sandy beaches with the waves. As a wave retreats, many mole crabs emerge from within the sand, scurry along with the wave, and then quickly reburrow.

Fascinating facts:

Whether it is digging in the sand, crawling along the beach, or swimming in the water, a mole crab always travels backward.

Periwinkles

What they look like:

Periwinkles have shells that grow unevenly into compact spirals. Most periwinkles are between $1/2$ and 1 inch long. They are some of the most common creatures on both the Pacific and Atlantic seashores.

Where they live:

Periwinkles are found throughout the world and are particularly plentiful in North America. They are common on rocks, among rockweeds, and in crevices and tide pools in all zones.

How to find them:

During calm periods they can be found grazing across algae-covered rocks. During times of high tidal activity, they will seek shelter under the edges of rocks or in rock crevices.

Fascinating facts:

Periwinkles were accidently introduced to North America from western Europe around 1860. Since then, they have become one of the most abundant organisms in coastal tide pools.

Periwinkle

One type of periwinkle, the Dogwinkle, drills through the shells of barnacles and mussels with its tongue.

Other High-Tide Organisms

black turban snail   green algae
hermit crabs   limpets
sea lettuce   shore crabs
springtails

 # Making a Seaweed Press

Collecting and drying seaweed can be a great way to learn about life in and around tide pools. The many varieties of seaweed can be dried, flattened, labeled, and assembled into an interesting collection and remembrance of a trip to a tide pool. You may wish to consult a good seaweed book to learn more about the different varieties.

You'll need:

hand or machine drill (have an adult help you)
2 sheets of plywood or fiberboard, 10 x 13 inches each
heavy white paper like oaktag or drawing paper
pieces of an old bedsheet
lots of newspapers
4 long bolts with wing nuts
2 8$^{1}/_{2}$ x 11-inch pieces of cardboard (cut from a box)

What to do:

1. Ask an adult to drill holes (to fit your bolts) in each corner of the 2 pieces of wood. The holes should be about 1 inch in from the top and side of each corner (drill the two boards *together,* and the holes will be sure to match up).
2. Put the connecting bolts through one board and lay it down so that the bolts stick upward.
3. Lay a piece of cardboard on top of this board.
4. Wet a sheet of heavy white paper and lay it on top of the cardboard.
5. Place a seaweed sample on top of the white paper.
6. Cover the seaweed with a piece of bedsheet.
7. Cover the cloth with a thick layer of newspaper.
8. Repeat steps 4–7 with other seaweed samples until you have mounted all the specimens you want to press.

9. Lay a second piece of heavy white paper on top of this pile.
10. Lay a second piece of cardboard on top of this pile.
11. Put the second piece of plywood on top of the last cardboard piece on the stack, threading the bolts through the holes.
12. Put a wing nut on each bolt and tighten them until you feel pressure. Then carefully tighten each bolt in turn as much as you can, putting even pressure on the stack.
13. Replace the wet newspapers with dry ones at least once each day.
14. After a week, carefully remove all the specimens from the press (the seaweed will be stuck to the white paper by a natural adhesive in the seaweed).
15. Label each of the specimens with its name, where it was collected, and the date of collection.

MID-TIDE ZONE

The organisms that live in this region of the shoreline are varied and colorful. They include a diverse collection of plants all struggling for places on the rocks, as well as a medley of animals that need to cling to those same rocks in order to obtain food and survive the constant crashing of waves.

This portion of the shoreline is covered by the tide for three-quarters of the day and exposed only at the lowest tides. That means that it is typically under water for about 18 hours and exposed to the air for approximately 6 hours each day.

This zone is frequently the most violent. There is lots of competition between organisms for places to live as well as competition for the food that ebbs and flows in and out of this environment. The constant crashing of waves also makes this a turbulent place for many organisms.

The *dominant* or *indicator* organisms for this zone are mussels and rockweeds.

Selected Mid-Tide Organisms

Sea Stars (Starfish)

What they look like:

Sea stars come in a wide variety of colors ranging from brown, black, red, yellow, and orange.

Their outer skin is usually rough in appearance. Some species may appear to have short, knobby spines all over their exteriors.

Most sea stars have 5 legs; a few varieties have as many as 50 legs.

Sea star

Where they live:

There are more than 5,000 different species of sea stars. They can be found in tide pools from Alaska to Baja California and from the Arctic to the Gulf of Mexico.

How to find them:

Sea stars cling under lower rock ledges, on rocky shelves, on seaweed mats, and in tiny crevices throughout a tide pool.

Fascinating facts:

If a sea star loses an arm or if an arm is damaged, a new one will grow in its place.

A sea star eats by pulling apart the shell of a clam or mussel and inserting its stomach inside the shell. The sea star secretes digestive juices inside the unlucky mollusk and digests it right inside its own shell.

Chitons

What they look like:

Chitons are *mollusks* (soft-bodied animals) that have 8 overlapping plates on their backs.

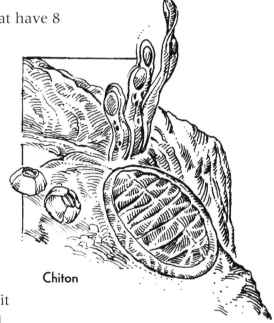

Chiton

Where they live:

About 100 different species occur along the Pacific Coast from Alaska to southern California.

A smaller number of species can be found along the Atlantic seaboard from the northern Atlantic to the tropics.

How to find them:

They usually creep on the undersides of rocks.

The flexibility of their plates allows them to fit snugly into crevices or depressions in and around rocks.

Fascinating facts:

Chitons eat by scraping their *radulae* (tongues) over the thin films of algae that coat the rocks where they live.

The Rough Chiton, which lives in tide pools in Washington, Oregon, and California, may live as long as 25 years.

Hermit Crabs

What they look like:

Hermit crabs have hard shells over the front part of their bodies and claws, but not over their soft, coiled abdomens (belly area). Consequently they need to slip into empty periwinkle or whelk shells to protect their backsides.

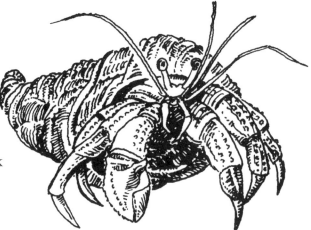

Hermit crab

Where they live:

They are very common in tide pools along both the Pacific and Atlantic shores.

How to find them:

They can be located scampering over and under rocks or across the sand as they forage for food (algae and very small creatures).

Fascinating facts:

As a hermit crab grows it needs to locate larger and larger shells to move into.

Other Mid-Tide Organisms

anemones	barnacles
limpets	mussels
pricklebacks	rockweed
sculpins	sea lettuce
sea palms	shore crabs
slipper shells	snail fur
sponges	springtails

LOW-TIDE ZONE

If any of the 3 zones could be called "peaceful" it would be this one. Because it is normally underwater, except for at extremely low tide (known as "minus tides"), the organisms that live here are less competitive and more cooperative. Fish, sponges, crabs, and kelp all live in harmony with one another.

This zone has one of the richest and most diverse assortment of organisms ever. The variety of plants and animals is incredible. Here you will discover animals that look like plants and plants that look like animals. You'll discover a host of strange and colorful creatures such as sea slugs, brittle stars, sea anemones, and octopi. You'll also find an enormous collection of flora (plants) such as hydroids, plankton, seaweeds, and algae.

The dominant, or indicator, organisms for this zone are sea anemones and kelp.

Selected Low-Tide Organisms

Kelp

What it looks like:

Instead of roots they have *holdfasts,* which anchor them to sand or rocks. What looks like a stem is called a *stipe.* The *blades* are similar to the leaves of a land plant.

Some seaweeds have little gas-filled bulbs, called *bladders,* that help them float.

Where it lives:

Kelp (often referred to as California giant kelp) is found primarily along the coast of California.

Other types of kelp, such as horsetail kelp, sugar kelp, and edible kelp, grow along the Atlantic seaboard from Maine to Rhode Island.

Kelp

How to find it:

Kelp can be located along most rocky shores where it grows attached to rocks, rocky ledges, shells, and other hard surfaces.

Fascinating facts:

In California, kelp is harvested by special boats, which "mow" it just a few feet below the surface of the water.

A chemical in kelp, known as *algin,* is used in some paints, cosmetics, toothpaste, chocolate milk, medicines, salad dressing, pudding, and even some ice cream.

Sea Anemones

What they look like:

Sea anemones look like flowers gently swaying in tidal waters. There are several species ranging in size from $1/2$ inch to over 18 inches tall.

The mouth is ringed by several rows of stinging tentacles. When disturbed or when feeding, they force water out of their body column, fold inward, and pull their tentacles and food in with them.

Where they live:

They can be found in the Pacific Ocean from Alaska to Southern California. In the Atlantic Ocean they are located from the Arctic down to North Carolina.

Sea anemone

How to find them:

Colonies of sea anemones can be easily located on large sections of rocks in and around tide pools. They also can be found on the pilings that support docks and piers.

Fascinating facts:

Some species of anemones have more than 1,000 tentacles.

The stinging cells in their tentacles can paralyze small fish. Other fish, such as the clown fish, can swim in and between their tentacles without being stung at all.

Other Low-Tide Organisms

abalones	algae
barnacles	hydroids
kelp snail	lampshells
lobsters	moon jellies
red algae	rock crabs
sand dollars	sculpins
sea hare	sea peach
spider crab	sponges
surf grass	urchins
whelks	

Visiting the seashore and examining the wide variety of life found in tide pools can be an exciting experience. You will learn much about the organisms that live and survive in this hectic and turbulent ecosystem. You also will gain an appreciation for one of the ocean's most important regions, and its value to life in the sea.

3 Coastal Oceans

The coastal seas of the world contain some of the most amazing life-forms found anywhere in the world. Some of these plants and animals live near the surface of the ocean, while others live way down in the depths—many strange and unusual organisms inhabit the deep and dark reaches of the planet. Interestingly, ocean plants can only be found in the upper reaches (what we call the sunlit zone) of the ocean, while animals and other sea creatures inhabit all layers of the ocean. The reason for this is quite simple: plants need sunlight to live and grow, and sunlight can only penetrate the upper layer of the ocean.

Scientists divide the ocean into 5 very broad and general areas or zones. These zones are separated by how far sunlight can penetrate the zone, the temperature of the water, and the organisms that live in that zone. The following illustration depicts these zones.

Sunlit Zone: This is the top layer in the ocean. It is named because there is plenty of sunlight in this part of the ocean. This is the layer where most ocean currents occur throughout the world. This layer is from sea level to a depth of approximately 660 feet. Organisms that live in this zone include sharks, seaweed, coral, turtle, jellyfish, tuna, herring, and whales.

Twilight Zone: This zone represents the maximum depth to which light penetrates the water. Typically, no plants grow in this zone. This zone ranges from a depth of 660 feet to 3,300 feet. Water temperatures here may go down to about 41°F. Animals that typically live in this region include sponges, octopi, some types of coral, some species of whales (e.g., sperm whales), and hatchet fish.

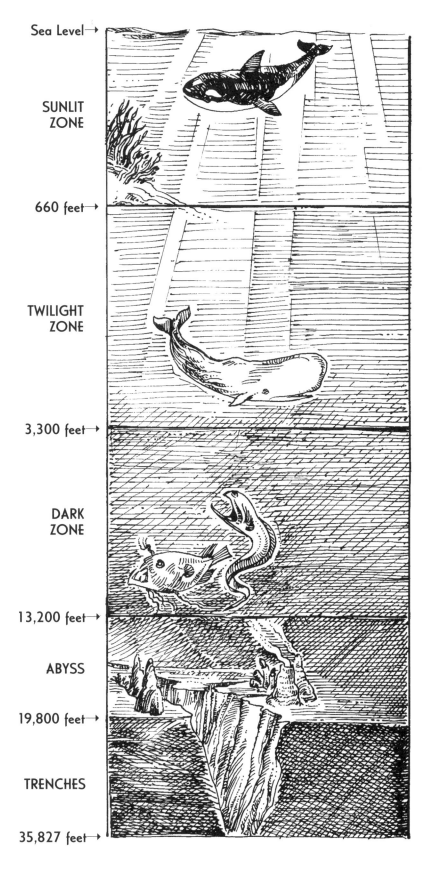

Sea Level →

SUNLIT ZONE

660 feet →

TWILIGHT ZONE

3,300 feet →

DARK ZONE

13,200 feet →

ABYSS

19,800 feet →

TRENCHES

35,827 feet →

Dark Zone: This zone ranges from a depth of 3,300 feet to about 13,200 feet. Water pressure increases tremendously and water temperatures range from 34–36°F. Animals in this part of the ocean include gulper eels, anglerfish, sea spiders, and rattail fish.

Abyss: This zone is without light and includes some of the deepest parts of the world's oceans (more than 13,200 feet in depth). Temperatures here are just above the freezing point and the animals that live in this region are some of the most unusual. Water pressure is tremendous, food is scarce, and much of the seabed is covered with mudlike oozes. Creatures such as sea cucumbers, brittle stars, tripod fish, and sea lilies live here.

Trenches: This is the deepest zone of the ocean. There are several trenches, or very deep canyons, on the ocean floor. These trenches are more than 19,800 feet below sea level (the world's deepest trench, the Mariana Trench, off the coast of the Philippines, is 36,200 feet deep).

22

What Is a Fish?

Fish are marvelous creatures! Over thousands of years they have evolved into some of the most amazing and distinctive organisms on earth. In fact, there are more than 25,000 different species of fish in the oceans, lakes, and rivers of the world. There are literally billions and billions of fish in every type of water environment. In the ocean, most fish live in the sunlit zone.

There are lots and lots of fish, but in spite of all those different varieties, most fish share some common physical features and characteristics. Let's take a look at some of them.

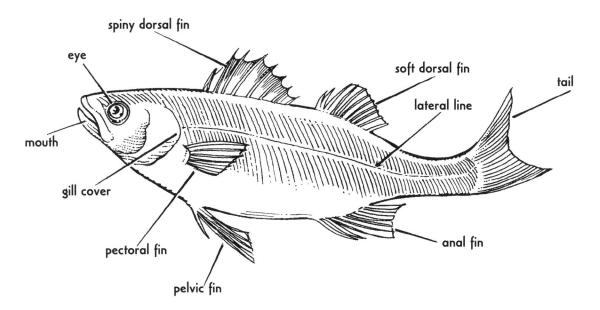

Mouth

A fish's mouth serves 2 purposes. It is what the fish uses to eat and what it uses to "breathe." A fish "breathes" by taking in water through its mouth. The water passes over the fish's gills. The gills remove the oxygen from the water and pass it into the bloodstream.

Scales

Most fish have a series of overlapping scales that help protect the fish (in many species of fish you can determine its age by counting the number of "rings" on an individual scale). A slimy substance, known as mucus, covers the scales. Mucus keeps the scales moist, protects the fish from infection, and helps the fish slip through the water faster.

23

Swim Bladder

The swim bladder is like a tiny balloon inside the fish. Fish use their swim bladders to keep themselves afloat. By changing the amount of air in their swim bladders, fish stay balanced in the water—never rising or sinking unless they want to.

Eyes

Most fish have very distinctive eyes. Fish eyes are round and very large (in proportion to their head). These eyes give them a wide field of vision. This is important because fish do not have necks and, thus, cannot turn their heads around like you or me.

Fins

Fins are essential to a fish's movement through the water. They help the fish to move forward, steer, and maintain balance. Here are the basic fins on most fish:

- Dorsal fin: This fin, on the top of the fish, keeps the fish from rolling over in the water.
- Pectoral fins: Located on the sides of the fish, these fins are used for balance, braking, and steering.
- Pelvic fin: Found underneath the fish, this single fin is also important in guiding the fish through the water and for helping it maintain its balance.
- Anal fin: This fin is located near the anus (rear end) of the fish. It works with the dorsal fin to help stabilize the fish.
- Caudal fin (or tail): At the very end of the fish is the tail fin. It is used to provide power to the fish by thrusting it through the water.

Gills

As previously mentioned, most fish have gills that help them take in oxygen from the water. These gills are protected by a gill cover—a bony plate known as the *operculum* that extends over the gills. Fish use special muscles to open and close their gill covers, thus "pumping" water constantly over the gills.

Lateral Line

The lateral line has often been referred to as a fish's "sixth sense." This remarkable mechanism allows a fish to sense movement or differences in water pressure. The lateral line is a row of sensory nerves along each side of the fish's body. Each lateral line runs from the head to the tail and is extremely sensitive to movement and pressure changes in the water.

24

 # Print-a-Fish

Here's a great activity that will help you learn about fish physiology. In fact, this activity has been practiced in Japan for more than 100 years.

You'll need:

1 whole fish (can be obtained from the fish department of most supermarkets)
newspaper
paper towels
newsprint (available from any art store or hobby store)
water-soluble paint (liquid tempera paint or artist's acrylic paint are both available from hobby, craft, or art stores)
artist's paint brushes
masking tape

What to do:

1. Wash the fish thoroughly with soap and water to remove any mucus.

2. Lay the fish on a sheet of newspaper. Paint one side of the fish with the paint (any color will do). If necessary, thin the paint with a few drops of water. Stroke the fish from tail to head (this allows ink to catch under the edges of scales and spines and will improve the print, especially if you use a thin coat of paint.

3. Paint the fins and tail last, since they tend to dry out quickly. Do not paint the eye.

4. If the newspaper under your fish becomes wet with ink during the painting process, move the fish to a clean sheet of newspaper before printing. Otherwise, your print will pick up leftover splotches of color.

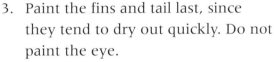

5. Carefully and slowly lay a sheet of newsprint over the fish. Taking care not to move the paper, use your hands and fingers to gently press the paper over the fish. Press the paper gently over the fins and tail. Be careful not to wrinkle the paper or you will get a blurred or double image.
6. Slowly and carefully peel the paper off. Paint in the eye with a small brush. Tape the print to a wall and allow to dry.

What happens:

You have created a fish print that you can display in your room or classroom. This is a traditional Japanese practice called gyotaku (pronounced ghio-ta-koo). It comes from two Japanese words (gyo = fish, taku = rubbing). This is one way Japanese people record their catches, and it has evolved into an art form throughout the world.

You may want to experiment with different types of paper for this activity. Thinner paper (tissue paper, rice paper) will provide a print that shows more details of the fish, but they tend to wrinkle much more easily when wet. Thicker paper (construction paper) is easier to handle, but does not provide a detailed print.

Note: You may need to practice this activity several times to get the technique down. Be patient and you will discover that the more you practice, the more intricate your fish prints will become.

Adaptation

There are millions and millions of creatures in the oceans of the world. That means that there are millions of creatures all competing for food and all trying to survive or avoid becoming food for someone else. To survive, it is often necessary for animals to have special body features, behaviors, or physical characteristics that allow them to obtain food or to avoid becoming food for someone else. In this section you'll learn about some shapes, behaviors, and body parts that are examples of adaptations and that are essential to the survival of selected ocean fish.

Shape

While animals, particularly ocean animals, come in a wide variety of shapes and sizes, there are basically 6 main shapes for fish. These are not the only shapes, but most of the fish you see at an aquarium, at a pet store, in the ocean, or even in your local supermarket will exhibit at least 1 of these basic shapes.

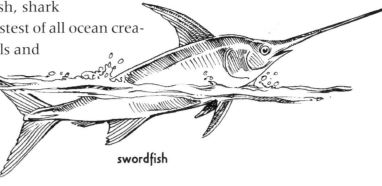

Fusiform: tuna, bluefish, swordfish, shark

Fish with this shape are the fastest of all ocean creatures. These fish have powerful tails and a torpedo-shaped body that "cuts" through the water very efficiently. Many of these fish live in open sea and swim continuously throughout their lifetimes.

swordfish

Sphere: puffer fish, balloon fish, porcupine fish

When they are threatened, these fish have the unique ability to swallow large quantities of water or air so their bodies swell up to 2 to 3 times their normal size. Other fish find it impossible to swallow these enlarged fish and thus leave them alone.

Rod: barracuda

These are the hunters of the oceans. Their thin, pencil-like shape allow them to hunt and ambush their prey with lightning speed. Typically, these fish like to float or lazily "cruise" through the water until a smaller fish swims nearby. Then they lunge, quickly and rapidly, to capture their next meal.

butterfly fish

Compressed: anglerfish, butterfly fish

When you look at these fish from the front you'll note that they seem to be pressed flat from side to side. These fish, typically found in tropical waters or coral reefs, are able to make quick turns and dart rapidly through the water.

Depressed: skate, ray, flounder, halibut

Unlike the compressed shape, these fish are flattened from top to bottom—often looking like dinner plates on the floor of the ocean. Along with their flattened shapes, they are also camouflaged to look like the sand or rocks on the ocean bottom.

Ribbon: wolf fish, eel

Their body shape makes them look like ribbons or streamers in the water. They can turn and bend easily up,

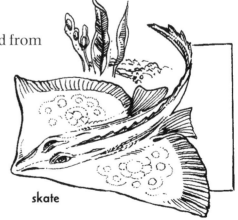

skate

over, and around rocks, through cracks and crevices, and in and out of small openings. They usually like to hide from other fish—darting out to ambush smaller fish that get too close.

conger eel

Coloration

The colors that a fish or species of fish have may help them to survive, avoid enemies, or enter into unusual relationships with other ocean creatures. A fish's color may help it hide from a predator, or it may be an aid in helping it capture its own food. Following are some typical color schemes used by fish.

Camouflage: plaice, pipefish, sargassum fish

Some fish are able to conceal themselves to avoid being eaten by their enemies. Other fish disguise themselves so that they can sneak up on their food and capture it. Scientists refer to this hiding ability as camouflage.

Warning: stonefish, scorpion fish, lionfish, puffer fish

Several fish, mostly in tropical areas, have a variety of colors, spines, poisons, and armors over and throughout their body. Their odd shapes, colors, and body appendages are designed as warnings to other animals: "Don't mess with me, I'm dangerous!"

scorpion fish

Disruptive: triggerfish

Different colors, spots, stripes, and distinctive markings on fish break up their body outline so that they are difficult to see in the water. These colorations make a fish hard to see, hard to locate, and hard to find in and around rocks, coral reefs, and undersea formations.

Advertising: cleaner wrasse

Cleaner wrasses perform a unique service for other, usually larger, fish. They nibble on the dead skin, parasites, and pests that are frequently on the surface of other fish. Their colors help identify them as beneficial fish and the larger fish leave them alone while they are performing their "clean up" service.

cleaner wrasse

Countershading: sharks, tuna

These fish have developed (over many thousands of years) a unique way of hiding. They have dark backs and light bellies. Viewed from above, the dark backs

appear to blend in with the darkness of the deep ocean. Viewed from below, their pale bellies appear to blend in with the sunlight streaming into the ocean. With this coloration, these fish can hunt for their prey without being easily seen.

False Eye Spots: butterfly fish, angelfish

Some tropical fish have developed spots near the back of their bodies that look amazingly like eyes—false eyes. These spots are often much larger than the fish's normal eyes. From certain angles the fish looks like it is much larger than it really is. Predators see this "eye" and think that they've encountered an enormous fish and will then leave it alone or allow it to escape in the opposite direction.

Two Coastal Creatures
Whales

Whales belong to a group of animals known as *Cetaceans*. This group also includes porpoises and dolphins. All of these creatures are also referred to as marine mammals and, just like other land mammals, they breathe air with lungs, have hair on some parts of their bodies, bear live young, nurse their young with milk produced by mammary glands, and maintain a constant internal body temperature.

All species of whales have a torpedo, or fusiform, body shape. As you have learned earlier in this chapter, a fusiform shape allows a sea creature to move through the water very efficiently. Additionally, whales' ears, limbs, mammary glands, and sex organs have all been streamlined in order to increase their efficiency in the water.

Whales are also noted for having a thick layer of blubber under the skin. This blubber aids buoyancy, provides a reserve energy source, and provides necessary insulation in cold waters.

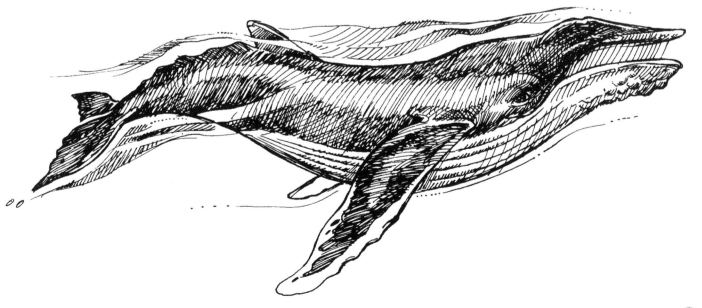

 # Warm Fat

This activity will help you appreciate the value of blubber as an important insulating substance.

You'll need:

>   1 container (a sink or bucket) of cold water
>   2 glass thermometers (drugstore thermometers work well)
>   1 package of suet or lard (available in any grocery store)

What to do:

1. **Note: This will be messy.** Get a handful of suet or lard and form it into a ball approximately 2 inches in diameter.
2. Place the bulb of one of the thermometers into the middle of the ball of suet or lard.
3. Clean off your hands with paper towels.
4. Place the thermometer without the suet or lard into the container of cold water. Place the other thermometer (with the suet or lard) into the same container.
5. Wait 15 minutes. Note the temperature reading on each of the 2 thermometers.

What happens:

You'll note that the temperature reading on the thermometer in the suet or lard ball has a higher reading than the other thermometer. This indicates that the suet or lard is *insulating* the bulb from the cold water.

Insulators (such as lard, suet, fat, or blubber) are materials that slow down the loss of heat from an object. Because whales are warm-blooded animals they produce their own heat to stay warm. Their layer of blubber reduces the transfer of heat from their body to the surrounding water. Blubber protects the whale and allows it to live in very cold water. Interestingly, in spite of thick layers of blubber, most whales tend to lose more heat than they produce. As a result, they need to swim constantly in order to stay warm.

Although all whales are air-breathing creatures, some whales can dive to great depths in the water and stay underwater for long periods of time. For example, sperm whales can swim to depths of 3,000 feet and remain underwater for almost an hour. Humans, on the other hand, can only free dive to a depth of about 33 feet and stay underwater for a maximum of 4 minutes.

Whales breath through the top of their heads with a blowhole, which consists of either 1 or 2 nostrils. Whales can open or close their blowholes at will, depending on whether they are underwater or above the surface of the water. When surfacing many whales are known to "blow their noses" or send a stream of water into the air from their blowholes.

Whale are grouped into 2 separate categories depending on what they eat:

Toothed whales are generally smaller whales with 1 blowhole on the top of their heads. Social animals, they usually travel in large groups, called pods, and feed on large groups of fish or squid, which they catch with sharp, cone-shaped teeth. Typically, they swallow their food whole or tear it into large chunks. They are also very fast swimmers.

Baleen whales are generally larger than toothed whales with 2 blowholes on the top of their heads. Solitary swimmers, they are considerably slower than toothed whales. These whales are distinguished by the fact that they do not have teeth, but rather a particular feeding structure known as *baleen*. Baleen is a flexible, fringed comb made of the protein keratin (the same material in your fingernails). This material hangs in rows from the whale's upper jaw and grows continuously throughout the whale's lifetime. As the whale swims through the water, small planktonic animals, such as krill, worms, and shrimp, become trapped in these sievelike plates and are swallowed by the whale.

The chart below lists several different species of whales according to how they eat.

Toothed Whales	Baleen Whales
bottlenose whales	blue whales
dolphins	brydes whales
killer whales	fin whales
narwhals	grey whales
pilot whales	humpback whales
porpoises	minke whales
sperm whales	right whales
white whales	sei whales

Fascinating Facts

- Most scientists believe that whales descended from a 4-legged land animal.
- Whales have been on earth for almost 60 million years.
- The blue whale is the largest animal that has ever lived; it's even larger than the largest dinosaur.
- A blue whale can weigh up to 280,000 pounds—that's 140 tons!
- Although they are mammals, whales have no surface hair on their skin.
- A sperm whale can stay underwater for up to 75 minutes and can dive to depths of 1,500 feet to search for food.
- Whale milk is so rich that a baby whale will double its weight in the first week of life.
- Depending on the species, whales will live anywhere from 30 to 70 years.
- The brain of a sperm whale weighs 20 pounds; the brain of an adult human being weighs 3 pounds.
- There are 40 different species of whales, many of which are on the endangered species list.
- The age of a toothed whale can be determined by cutting a tooth lengthwise. Each "ring" indicates a year of life.
- Adult beluga whales are pure white in color. They also make chirping noises similar to birds.

Whales are found in most of the oceans of the world. However, several species of whales are endangered or threatened. That means that if humans continue to hunt these whales for food or other materials they may die out altogether. Although several countries have enacted bans or limits on whale hunting, indiscriminate killing still occurs on the high seas where it is often difficult to enforce laws. If you are interested in learning more about how you can help protect the whales of the world (as well as "adopt" a whale of your own) write to:

International Wildlife Coalition
Whale Adoption Project
634 North Falmouth Highway
P.O. Box 388
North Falmouth, MA 02566

OR

Pacific Whale Foundation
101 North Kihei Road
Kihei, HI 96753
(808) 870-8860

Note: Here's a terrific website that focuses on whales and whale research. You can ask scientists questions, gather important information about various whale species, and electronically track whale movements and migrations: http://whale.wheelock.edu.

Sharks

Sharks are part of a class of fish known as *Chondrichthyes*. Fish in this class all have a skeleton made of cartilage (the same material as your nose and ears). This compares with most other fish whose skeletons are made of bone. However, just like bony fish, this class of fish has jaws, paired fins, and paired nostrils. Another recognizable feature of these fish is their torpedo shape and their 5 to 7 pairs of gill slits.

Sharks are well adapted to life in the sea—particularly life as a predator. Most sharks are countershaded—with a dark back that, when seen from above, blends in with the darker depths of the ocean. They also have white bellies that, when seen from below, blends in with the sunlight streaming down from the surface. Several species also have a distinctive array of spots and stripes, which further help them blend in with their surroundings.

Sharks have been the subject of countless books and scores of horrifying movies. They are wrapped in mystery and surrounded by superstition and myth. In fact, many primitive people honor and revere the shark for its power and ferociousness. Indeed, sharks have always been fascinating to humans, even though we know very little about them.

Much of the fear of sharks comes from reports of shark attacks on humans (the great white shark being the most recognizable "villain"). However, statistics show that only about 5 to 10 people per year are killed worldwide by sharks. Also interesting is the fact that of the 350 different species of sharks only 32 species have been known to attack humans. Also, over 80 percent of all shark species are less than 6 feet long, and 50 percent of all sharks are less than 3 feet long.

When a shark grabs on to its prey and begins biting down, its teeth are frequently knocked out. As soon as a tooth falls out it is quickly replaced by another tooth. In fact, a shark's jaw is similar to a miniature conveyor belt with teeth constantly being replaced. Some species of shark may lose as many as 2,000 teeth a year or 30,000 teeth in a lifetime.

Fascinating Facts

- Almost 70 percent of a shark's brain is used for the sense of smell.
- Special organs in a shark's lip (called the ampullae or Lorenzini) can pick up electrical impulses.
- Sharks can hear sounds in the water that are more than a half mile away.
- Deep-water sharks have larger eyes than shallow-water sharks.
- Sharks are considered the first living creatures to develop teeth.
- Many species of sharks are actually afraid of people.
- Sharks can detect 1 drop of blood in 100,000 gallons of water.
- Sharks have a 2-chambered heart; humans have a 4-chambered heart.

- Sharks don't eat very often. In fact, some sharks only eat once a month.
- Some sharks are not very discriminating in what they eat. Some things they have eaten include crocodiles, horses, cows, dogs, cats, alarm clocks, bicycles, ship propellers, and torpedoes.
- The scales of a shark (called *dermal denticles*) have the same structure as a human tooth.
- In clear water, sharks can only see effectively for about 50 feet.
- The smallest shark in the world is the dwarf shark, which reaches a total length of 6 inches.

Some scientists believe that sharks are essential to the ecological balance of the ocean. They often feed on dying, sick, or injured animals, thus ensuring healthy populations of many species of ocean life. If some species of sharks are eliminated or eradicated, the ecology of the ocean could be seriously affected or altered.

Note: Here's an incredible website that has loads of fascinating information about sharks. You can e-mail scientists, look up information about various species of sharks (including the great white shark), and link up with other websites. Don't miss the accompanying music on this site: http://users.bart.nl/~jkoetze/.

The coastal creatures you have met above are just a few of the many thousands of living organisms that can be found in the coastal seas of the world. This area of the ocean has the richest variety of sealife as well as some of the most distinctive and unusual species of plants and animals anywhere on the earth. To learn more about these amazing organisms, you may wish to consult the list of children's literature in chapter 9.

4 Into the Depths

Imagine living in a world where there is very little light or no light at all! Imagine trying to locate your food in the dark. Imagine trying to travel from one place to another without the benefit of lights. Imagine trying to survive with hundreds of pounds of pressure on all parts of your body.

This world exists—it exists far below the surface of the ocean. It is a world filled with incredible creatures, unexplainable events, and eye-popping discoveries. It is a world divided into several zones—each with its own unique animals, mysteries, and features. Let's take a trip through this magical world.

The Twilight Zone

As discussed in chapter 3, this region of the ocean ranges from 660 feet to 3,300 feet below sea level. It is called the twilight zone because very little light penetrates the water at these depths. In fact, only cold blue light is able to reach this far down. In this dim existence many marine creatures are bioluminescent—that is, they harbor colonies of special bacteria that produce chemical reactions that generate light. This bioluminescence is used in different ways by different organisms. Some creatures send out light flashes in order to attract mates in the darkness, some fish blind their predators with quick and bright flashes of light, and other organisms use light organs on the underside of their bodies to camouflage themselves. Let's take a look at some of these incredible creatures.

Flashlight Fish

This amazing fish has light organs underneath each of its eyes. These organs contain glowing bacteria that help the fish locate food and communicate with other

flashlight fish. The fish also has special covers (similar to eyelids) that it can use to cover up the light, which gives it the ability to turn the light organs on and off.

Lanternfish

This is one of the most common fish in the twilight zone. It gets its name from the rows of light organs that run along the sides and underside of its body.

lanternfish

Viperfish

This fish gets its name from its long needlelike fangs and its snake-like body. A fearsome looking fish, it only grows to about 10 inches in length. Not only does it have rows of lights along its body, but it also has a slender spine that hangs in front of its mouth with a tiny light at the end—a light that is used to attract smaller fish into its mouth.

Hatchetfish

This strange looking fish has several light organs underneath its body. These organs confuse any would-be predators that might be swimming beneath them. Besides their light organs, hatchetfish have enormous eyes that can pick up the faint glow of small fish and shellfish.

hatchetfish

Anglerfish

The female anglerfish has a luminous lure that hangs out and over her mouth. The luminescent bacteria within this light organ helps attract fish to the anglerfish. The anglerfish is also noteworthy because of its expandable stomach. With its enormous jaw and oversized stomach this fish can swallow prey that is nearly twice as large as it is.

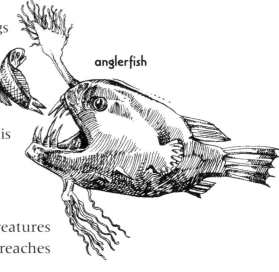

anglerfish

Glass Jellyfish

Found throughout the oceans of the world, these creatures are found in the twilight zone as well as in the upper reaches

of the sea. Like other jellyfish they have a deep bell from which hang long, sting-ing tentacles. Most spectacular, however, is their ability to display a rainbow of flashing colors while drifting through the water.

Water Pressure

Pressure is defined as a force applied over a certain area. Because of both the weight and density of water, water exerts pressure on its inhabitants. (Those of us who live at sea level experience air pressure at a force of 14.7 pounds per square inch. This measurement is known as *one atmosphere.*) The deeper organisms live in the ocean the greater the water pressure on them. In other words, water pressure increases equally with depth.

Underwater, pressure increases by one atmosphere for every 33 feet of depth. That means that at sea level the water pressure is about 14.7 pounds per square inch. At 33 feet below the surface of the ocean the water pressure is now two atmospheres or twice that at sea level (2 x 14.7 = 29.4 pounds per square inch). At 66 feet below sea level the water pressure is three atmospheres (3 x 14.7 = 44.1 pounds per square inch). In the twilight zone the water pressure ranges from about 294 pounds per square inch to 1,470 pounds per square inch. While certain ani-mals have adapted to those tremendous pressures, humans would be flattened instantly at those depths. At the bottom of the Mariana Trench, which is 35,827 feet below sea level (the deepest point on earth), the water pressure is 14,622.94 pounds per square inch.

The Darkest Depths

In this region of the ocean there is absolutely no light (light cannot penetrate more than 3,300 feet below sea level). This is a black world: the deepest, darkest part of the ocean filled with strange inhabitants with equally strange habits. A place where there is little food, frigid waters, and incredible pressures.

But many different kinds of amazing and bizarre animals live in this region. Let's examine a few.

Gulper Eel

The gulper eel has enormous jaws, which it can unhinge to open its im-mense mouth even wider. It can swim through the water with its mouth wide open scooping up anything and everything in its path. At the end of its tail is a tiny light organ that glows pink and red. This "lure" is used to attract small fish and tiny crustaceans into its waiting jaws.

Sea Cucumber

These creatures look like soft, squishy, slimy land slugs; however, they are related to sea stars (starfish). They crawl along the ocean floor feeding on the remains of dead animals and plants they find in the ooze.

Whipnose

Although only about 5 inches long, this unusual fish has a long "fishing line" extending from its nose. This line is more than twice the length of the fish and is used to lure its prey into its mouth.

Giant Sea Spider

This sea spider, with its tremendously long legs (they have a leg span of 2 feet across), crawls over the soft ooze of the sea bed. It has a long proboscis (feeding tube) which it injects into the sides of soft-bodied animals such as worms and sucks out their insides.

Tripod Fish

This fish gets its name from the 3 extra-long fins that it uses to hold itself above the ocean floor. From this position it waits for any passing fish to swim by. If a prey gets too close, the tripod fish pounces on it and eats it.

tripod fish

Halosaur

This bottom-dwelling fish is one of the longest at this depth. It grows to a length of more than 6 feet, which includes a sharply pointed snout and a long tapering body. It uses its snout to dig in the soft ooze looking for invertebrates and other sea creatures on the sea floor.

A wide variety of sea creatures live in the inky black depths of the ocean where the water pressure is incredible. The following chart lists several undersea creatures and the maximum depths (and corresponding water pressures) at which these animals have been discovered.

Animal	Greatest Depth (in feet)	Water Pressure (in pounds per square inch)
Barnacle	25,846	11,513
Prawn	20,903	9,311
Sea Anemone	35,194	15,677
Sea Cucumber	35,194	15,677
Sea Snail	35,053	15,614
Sea Spider	24,174	10,768
Sea Star	32,767	14,596
Sea Urchin	24,075	10,724
Sponge	32,767	14,596

Fantastic Fact

The greatest depth at which a fish has been seen underwater is 35,788 feet. At that depth the water pressure is nearly 8 tons per square inch.

The Ocean Floor

The ocean floor is a dark, cold, and foreboding place. Vast abyssal plains stretch for enormous distances with an occasional deep sea trench breaking up the landscape. Occasionally, there are hills, seamounts, and volcanoes sprinkled across this immense area, but mostly it is nothing more than flat stretches of sea bottom covered with a thick layer of deep, muddy ooze, which ranges in depth from 984 to 1,640 feet thick.

The temperature in this region of the ocean never rises to more than just above the freezing point and, of course, there is absolutely no light. No plants grow in this region because there is no light, consequently animals that live here must be able to filter and sift the water and mud from the ocean floor to locate tiny particles of food that have floated down from the upper layers of the ocean. Most of these food particles are the remains of dead animals and plants that sink from above. Let's look at a few of these amazing creatures.

Sea Pens

Sea pens are actually soft-bodied corals and are quite common along the floor of the ocean. They look like old-fashioned quill pens from which they get their name. They often grow to heights of 5 feet or more.

Sea Lilies

These creatures look like miniature feather dusters or underwater tropical plants, but they're really animals. They use their feathery arms to gather and filter tiny food particles from the surrounding water. Some species of sea lilies have special "roots," which they use to anchor themselves to the seabed.

Glass Sponges

These flower-shaped sponges are another common animal on the ocean floor. They grow to a height of 16 inches or more and are raised up off the sea floor by a thin stalk of twisted silica—a material very similar to fiberglass.

Brittle Stars

One of the most common groups of animals found on the sea bed are *echinoderms* (spiny-skinned animals). This group includes sea stars (starfish), sea urchins, and sea cucumbers. Brittle stars are noted for their long snakelike arms, which they use to cling to the ocean bottom and capture food particles floating by. Many brittle stars are found at depths of 330 to 5,940 feet.

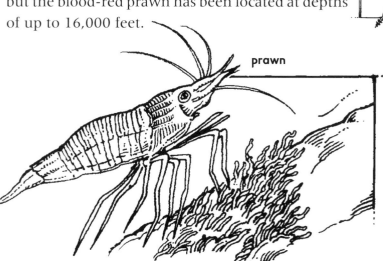

brittle star

Prawns

Prawns are similar in size and shape to shrimp. Several different species live in all zones of the ocean, but the blood-red prawn has been located at depths of up to 16,000 feet.

prawn

Many parts of the ocean bottom (particularly in the Pacific Ocean) are littered with a vast array of volcanoes, seamounts, and guyots. Oceanic volcanoes typically form in one of three ways:

- "Hot spot" volcanoes are those that form when a column of magma (hot lava) rises up through a break in the earth's crust.
- Ocean volcanoes form when 2 plates of the earth's crust begin to move apart. Magma oozes up to fill the gap between the plates.
- A third type of ocean volcano happens when a crustal plate slides under another like a giant conveyor belt. An erupting "hot spot" volcano is then "moved" across the floor of the ocean. This process, which occurs over many millions of years, is how thousands of volcanic islands have been created. The Hawaiian Islands (which are actually a chain of about 130 islands stretching more than 1,500 miles across the Pacific Ocean) were created over a period of 70 million years.

Blow Your Top

There are thousands of volcanoes on the ocean floor. This activity, although it doesn't take place underwater, will simulate the eruption of an undersea volcano.

You'll need:
1 20-ounce plastic soda bottle
lots of dirt
1 tablespoon liquid detergent
red food coloring
1 cup of vinegar
warm tap water
2 tablespoons of baking soda

What to do:
1. Take the bottle outside and place it on the ground. Mound up dirt around the sides of the bottle into a conical shape (the shape of a cone volcano).
2. Put 1 tablespoon of liquid detergent into the bottle.
3. Add a couple of drops of red food coloring.
4. Add 1 cup of vinegar.
5. Add warm tap water—filling the bottle almost to the top.
6. Mix 2 tablespoons of baking soda with a little water and add it very quickly to the bottle.

What happens:

In this activity the baking soda reacts with the vinegar to create a chemical reaction (carbon dioxide is produced). Since carbon dioxide gas is heavier than air it pushes the air out of the bottle. The detergent in the bottle helps create more bubbles and the food coloring make the "eruption" more spectacular.

Although undersea volcanoes don't have the same "ingredients" as in this activity, their behavior is somewhat similar. In an underwater volcano, however, hot molten rock (*magma*) rises up from deep inside the earth. This magma pushes through holes or cracks in the earth's crust and solidifies. With each eruption more and more magma builds up. In some places volcanoes continue to grow until they eventually break the surface of the ocean and form islands. The Hawaiian Islands are the tops of undersea volcanoes that grew higher and higher over millions of years of lava eruptions.

Vents and Smokers

In 1977 scientists studying the floor of the Pacific Ocean made an incredible discovery. They discovered cracks in the seabed from which hot, mineral-rich water was gushing. Just as remarkable was the fact that the water issuing from these vents was more than $700°$F and that it contained high concentrations of dissolved sulphur. Interestingly, sulphur is extremely poisonous to most organisms, yet the scientists also discovered an amazing array of several different and very unusual sea creatures, including the following:

- Giant tube worms were glowing in enormous clusters around these hot water vents. The worms, many longer than 10 feet, have thick colonies of bacteria living in their bodies. This bacteria is able to convert the hydrogen sulfide from the vents into food for themselves and the worms.
- Giant clams were found in and around these vents. Many of these were 12 inches or more in length and, like the tube worms, used bacteria in their gut to create food.
- Other crustaceans found around the vents included squat crabs and lobsters. These perfectly white animals are completely blind with no eyes in their eye sockets. They spend their lives foraging for small scraps of food stirred up by the rushing hot water.
- One of the most unusual animals discovered in these regions is the siphonophore. This animal looks just like a dandelion without a stalk. It has several threadlike tentacles that it anchors on the seabed while it floats several inches off the bottom. Its closest relative is the jellyfish.

As the superheated water issues forth from these sea vents it begins to deposit sulphur and other minerals around the sides of the vents. These build up over time to form tall chimneys (or "smokers")—often reaching heights of nearly 33 feet. These are also referred to as "black smokers," because all the sulphur being discharged by these chimneys colors the surrounding water black.

Exploring the Oceans

Since the beginning of recorded time people have always wanted to explore the vast reaches of the world's oceans. The length and breadth of the ocean's surface and the variety of underwater life and formations have always fascinated human beings. The mysteries of the deep waters, undersea wrecks and sunken treasures, and marine products, such as oil and sponges, have also been part of the lure of the ocean. Ever since the invention of the first diving bell by Edmund Halley in 1690,

humans have sought variety of methods and devises with which they could examine the world under the waves.

The first submarines were not invented to explore the ocean depths, but rather were used as instruments of war. A one-man wooden submarine, the *Turtle,* was used during the Revolutionary War (only once) to attach an exploding mine to the hull of an enemy ship. Since then a variety of other underwater vehicles have been invented allowing humans to probe deeper and deeper into the ocean. The chart below shows the depths and dates of some of these undersea vessels.

Vehicle/Invention	Date	Depth
Aqualung	1943	165 feet
Cousteau's Diving Saucer	1959	1,350 feet
JIM	1971	2,000 feet
NR-1	1969	2,300 feet
Bathysphere	1934	3,028 feet
DSRV-1	1965	5,000 feet
Cyana	1959	9,800 feet
Alvin	1964	12,500 feet
Bathyscaphe	1954	13,125 feet
Trieste	1953	35,813 feet
Archimède	1962	36,000 feet

Submarine Time

Here's a simple devise you can make, which will help you understand how a submarine works.

You'll need:

    1 tall glass or 1-quart canning jar
    eyedropper
    water
    large rubber balloon
    rubber bands

What to do:

1. Fill the glass jar with water up to about $^1/_2$ inch from the top.
2. Place the eyedropper into the water with enough water in it so that it barely floats (you may have to experiment several times to get just the right amount of water inside the eyedropper).
3. Cut off the neck of the balloon and stretch it tightly over the top of the jar. Secure the balloon to the neck of the jar with one or more rubber bands.
4. Push down on the balloon. Note how the eyedropper "submarine" descends into the water.
5. Pinch the balloon slightly in the middle and lift it up slowly. Notice how the "submarine" rises in the water.

What happens:

You'll notice that the "submarine" dives each time you press down on the balloon and that it rises each time you pull up on the balloon. When you push down you are increasing the air pressure (slightly) inside the jar. This increase in air pressure forces more water into the eyedropper, making it heavier. As a result, it sinks toward the bottom of the jar. When you raise the balloon, the air pressure is decreased inside the jar. As a result, the "submarine" becomes lighter and rises toward the surface. This device is sometimes called a "cartesian diver," and it uses the same principles as a submarine.

When the captain of a real submarine wants to go deeper in the water the order is given to fill special tanks (called ballast tanks) in the submarine with water. The weight of the water causes the submarine to sink. To rise to the surface, the water in the ballast tanks is forced out, thus making the submarine lighter and more buoyant.

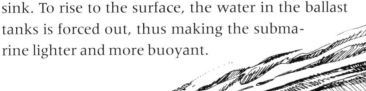

45

Modern Exploration

Major modern-day advances in technology and electronics have spawned a whole new generation of oceanic research. Now scientists, armed with the latest equipment and machinery, can explore every region, every zone, and every square inch of the ocean. This research is providing us with many incredible discoveries and enhancing our knowledge and appreciation of life beneath the waves.

While numerous discoveries are being made with submersibles and other manned vessels, some of the most important information is being collected by a wide assortment of undersea devises, some of which are listed below.

- *Echo sounders* are used to accurately measure the depth of water.
- *Box corers* are mechanical devises used for taking samples of the seabed for laboratory analysis.
- *Nansen bottles* are used to collect different water samples at various depths.
- *Benthic sled,* which is lowered to the sea bottom and with a series of nets is used to collect samples of sea animals.
- *Salinometers* are instruments used to calculate the salinity, or saltiness, of sea water.
- *GLORIA* stands for Geological Long-Range Inclined Asdic—a sonar devise that scans the seabed and maps it for scientists.
- *Current meter* is an instrument that calculates the speed and direction of water currents.
- *Camera sleds* are specially designed underwater sleds loaded with a variety of still cameras and video cameras. They are used to map the deepest parts of the ocean.
- *Satellites* are used to survey the ocean, detect wave patterns, measure surface temperature, track warm-water and cold-water currents, and monitor ocean pollution.

These inventions and underwater devises have added immeasurably to increase our knowledge about the oceans. As we probe deeper and deeper into the ocean depths, new devises will be created to help us gather important and valuable information about our watery world. Who knows, maybe you'll be one of those inventors or one of the new breed of oceanographers making fantastic discoveries in oceans near and far.

Top to Bottom

You may be wondering how scientists are able to map the ocean floor even when they can't see the bottom. This activity will simulate exactly how oceanographers used to do that many years ago before the invention of modern-day sonar equipment.

You'll need:

> large watertight Styrofoam cooler
> waterproof marker
> paper tags (see below)
> water
> blue or green food coloring
> bricks, rocks, gravel, and
>   sand (see below)
> 2 long thin strips of wood
>   (or 2 yardsticks)
> string
> yardstick
> metal washers
> data sheet (see page 48)

What to do:

1. Place bricks, rocks, gravel, and sand in the bottom of the Styrofoam cooler to make mountains, trenches, and plains (don't clutter the bottom with too many items). The items must be heavier than water so they don't float to the top.
2. Carefully fill the Styrofoam cooler with water to 1 inch from the top.
3. Put enough food coloring in the water to turn it a dark color (you should not be able to see the items on the bottom).
4. Use the yardstick to put marks 1 inch apart on all four edges of the interior walls of the cooler (see the accompanying illustration).

Data Sheet

North

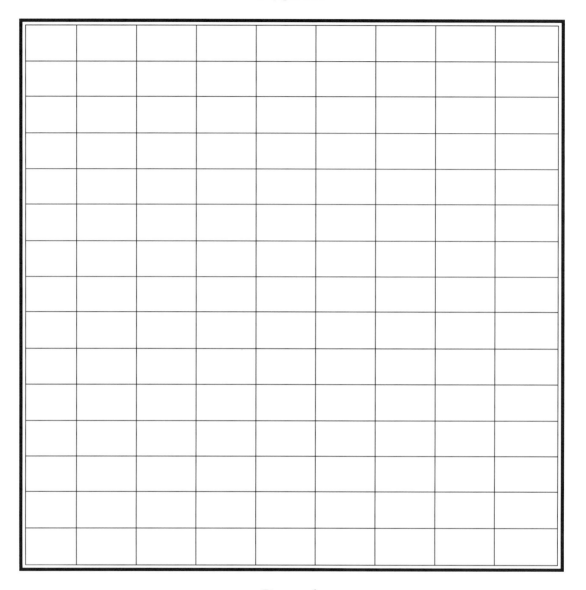

South

Write the depth at each "sounding" next to the position where the lines (and the dowels) cross. Record the depths from markings on the string.

Note: The data sheet is like a miniature "map" of the cooler as it might appear if you were looking straight down on the cooler. The marks on the sides of the cooler correspond to the 1-inch marks on the data sheet.

5. Write NORTH, SOUTH, EAST, and WEST on the sides of the cooler so that it will correspond to the directions on the data sheet. Using pins and paper tags marked with a waterproof pen, put tags every inch in each direction with A, B, C's going north to south and 1, 2, 3's going east to west across the cooler.

6. Tie 2 metal washers to a piece of string. Use the waterproof marker to make lines on the string $^1/_2$ inch apart.

7. Lay one of the thin wood strips widthwise on top of the cooler; lay the other strip lengthwise. The two strips have now formed a set of coordinates on top of the cooler (see the first illustration).

8. Dip the weighted string into the water at the junction of the first two coordinates.

9. Note the marking on the string when it hits something underneath the surface of the water. Mark that location (or depth) on the data sheet by writing the depth (in inches), read from the string markings, next to the position where those same two lines cross on the data sheet. Repeat for every set of 1-inch coordinates on the sides of the cooler and on the data sheet (you will need to move the wood strips each time).

10. When finished, you will have a "map" of the floor of your miniature "ocean." You may wish to carefully siphon the water from the cooler and compare your data sheet with the actual contours of your "ocean floor."

What happens:

Each time you dipped the string into the water it touched something on the bottom of the cooler. It may have been a tall object or a short object or no object at all. The markings on the string (and on your data sheet) tell you how deep each object is.

Before the invention of SONAR, oceanographers used to plot the ocean with instruments similar to the one you used in this activity. Weighted marked lines were lowered into the water from the deck of a ship. When the weight hit something the marking on the line indicated how deep that object or geological formation was.

SONAR is able to measure the ocean bottom very accurately and in much less time. Sound waves are sent down into the water, and the time it takes for the sound to travel to the bottom and bounce back to the ship is measured. In deeper parts of the ocean the sound takes longer to bounce back than it does in shallow places. With SONAR, scientists have been able to make very detailed maps of most of the oceans of the world.

5 Winds, Waves, and Currents

Look at the surfer in the illustration to the left. He is surfing down the front of a wave that may have been created hundreds of miles away by winds blowing across the surface of the sea. In fact, most waves are caused by the action of wind blowing across open expanses of the ocean. As the wind blows across the ocean, a series of small rounded waves (known as ripples) are set into motion. As the wind continues to blow, the ripples grow larger and turn into waves. These waves become longer and steeper as long as the wind continues to blow and they continue to move across the surface of the water.

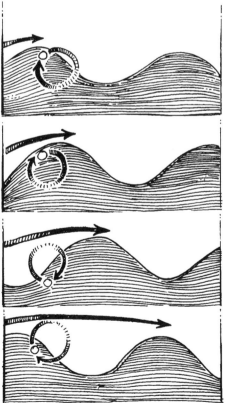

The water molecules in a wave do not move forward with the wave. Instead, each water molecule moves up and down (just like a bottle bobs up and down in the water) in a circular motion—ending up in approximately the same position as where it began (see the illustration to the right).

The wave moves through the water like the ripples in a rope if you tied one end of the rope to a chair and gave the other end a shake.

 Around and Around

This activity will help you understand how water molecules "behave" in a wave.

You'll need:

a small balloon
string
a large metal bolt
a deep roasting pan
water
an empty soda pop can

What to do:

1. Blow up the balloon to about the size of your closed fist. Tie off the neck.
2. Tie a piece of string to the neck of the balloon. The string should be about 12 inches long. Tie the other end of the string to the metal bolt.
3. Fill the large roasting pan with about 4 inches of water.
4. Place the bolt in the middle of the pan. The balloon should float on the surface of the water.
5. Float the empty soda pop can on the surface of the water at one end of the pan. Push up and down on the can to create waves in the water.
6. Notice what is happening to the balloon each time a wave passes under it.

What happens:

You'll note that the balloon moves in a circle around the metal bolt. The balloon is actually simulating the movement of water molecules in a wave. As a wave moves through the water, the water molecules do not move in a straight line, but rather move around and around in a circle within the wave. The diameter of the orbit of that circle is identical to the height of the wave.

Wave height is measured from a wave's *trough* (lowest point) to its *crest* (highest point). Interestingly, waves are not measured from the front, but rather at the back of the wave. That's why most waves look much higher than their actual measurement. A 3-foot wave (as measured from the back), for example, may look like a 6-foot wave from the front. Wave height is dependent on how far a series of waves has been "pushed" across the ocean and the strength and duration of the wind "pushing" those waves.

Another way of measuring the height of waves is with the Beaufort Scale. This scale, developed in the early 1800s, is used to indicate the strength of wind at sea. The scale uses the numbers from 0 to 12 to show how strong the wind is. Following is the Beaufort Scale and the effect of wind speed on wave height.

Beaufort Scale #	Wind Speed (mph)	Wave Height
0	less than 1	flat
1	1–3	ripples
2	4–7	small wavelets
3	8–12	
4	13–18	4 feet
5	19–24	
6	25–31	10 feet
7	32–38	
8	39–46	
9	47–54	25 feet
10	55–63	
11	64–75	
12	75+	46 feet

 Ocean Motion

Here's an activity that will give you an opportunity to create "homemade" waves and to watch their action in a bottle.

You'll need:

an empty 1-liter soda bottle (with a screw-on top)
vegetable oil
water
blue food coloring

What to do:

1. Fill an empty 1-liter soda bottle $^2/_3$ of the way up with water dyed with a few drops of blue food coloring.
2. Fill the rest of the bottle (all the way to the brim) with vegetable oil.
3. Put on the top securely and lay the bottle on its side. Now, slowly and gently rock the bottle back and forth by lifting the top then lifting the bottom.

What happens:

The oil in the bottle will begin to roll and move just like the waves in the ocean. You have created a miniature ocean in a bottle.

Waves are energy that moves through water. It is not the water that moves, but rather the energy in the water that causes waves to form. Ocean waves are generated by the gravitational pull of the moon on the earth's surface, the geological formation of the ocean floor, *and* the movement of wind across the surface of the water. You can artificially create waves in a soda bottle and observe wave action that is quite similar to that which occurs throughout the oceans of the world.

The distance between two waves is known as the *wavelength*. This distance is usually measured horizontally from the crest of one wave to the crest of another wave. Wavelength will vary from a few feet to a few hundred yards.

Most waves are caused by the action of wind on water; however, sometimes undersea disturbances, such as earthquakes, landslides, or volcanoes, can also create waves. These long, high-speed waves are known as *tsunamis* (soo-nah-mees) or tidal waves (actually "tidal waves" is the wrong terminology since these waves aren't created or affected by the tides). The speed of a tsunami can be as fast as 500 mph and the wavelength may be as much as 124 miles. Interestingly, the height of these waves is rarely more than 20 inches. However, as they near land they rear up (often to great heights of 95 feet or more), sucking up water. They then crash forward into the shore causing enormous damage and destruction.

Fantastic Fact

The largest tsunami on record occurred in 1971 off Ishigaki Island in Japan. It was an amazing 278 feet high.

Changing the Shoreline

As a wave nears the shore, the ocean floor begins to slope upward and the water becomes shallower. When the water molecules in the trough of the wave begin to hit against the land, friction slows their motion. At the same time, however, the molecules at the top (crest) of the wave are continuing to move at their same rate. The point at which this happens is typically when the water becomes less than half a wavelength deep. It's here that waves begin to build up. Eventually they topple over and crash on the beach. This constant breaking action is referred to as surf.

Over time, the ceaseless breaking action of the surf wears away large rocks and breaks them down into smaller and smaller rocks. Eventually, these small rocks will be further broken down into particles of sand. Obviously, this process takes many hundreds or thousands of years depending on the type of rock or mineral.

The pounding surf also moves the sand on the beach from place to place. Storms, large waves, and wind carry the sand from one spot to another on the beach or they may wash large quantities of sand out to sea. In many parts of the world (the East Coast of the United States, for example) this is an annual cycle. Beaches build up during the spring and summer months, and are often washed away by severe storms and waves action during the fall and winter months. Towns and communities spend large sums of money to erect barriers or to haul in new sand to rebuild their beaches each year.

Wash Away

Here's a simple activity that will demonstrate what happens when waves constantly hit the shore.

You'll need:
a paint roller pan
sand
water
an empty soda pop can

What to do:
1. Put enough sand in the paint roller pan to cover the entire bottom to a depth of about 1 inch.
2. Pour water very slowly into the deep end of the pan until it reaches about two-thirds of the way up the "beach." Be carefully not to disturb the sand.

3. Float the soda pop can on its side in the deep part of the pan. Grasp it with your fingers and push it up and down in the water to create waves.
4. Note the action of the waves as they roll across the surface or the "ocean" and up onto the "beach."

What happens:

As the waves hit the "beach" they move the sand down into the water. As more and more waves hit the "beach," more and more sand is washed down. If the waves are moving fast, more sand is being washed away than if the waves are moving slowly. By the same token, larger waves cause more erosion than smaller waves.

In nature, waves are pounding on the coastline constantly. Faster, bigger waves cause more of the sand to wash back into the ocean than slower, smaller waves. The slope of the shoreline will also affect how rapidly the sand washes away. Severe storms and hurricanes also tear up large expanses of shoreline—washing large quantities of sand back into the ocean.

Ocean Currents

Ocean water is never still—it is constantly moving in enormous "rivers" called currents. These currents move as gigantic belts of water at about 2–3 mph. In the Northern Hemisphere they move in a clockwise direction; in the Southern Hemisphere currents move in a counterclockwise direction. This phenomenon is called the *Coriolis effect.* One of the most well-known currents in the world is the Gulf

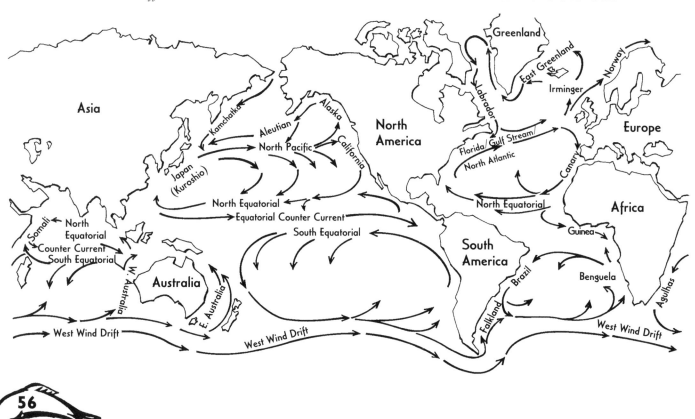

Stream, which carries warm water from the Caribbean up the East Coast of the United States, across the northern Atlantic, and over to the west coasts of England and Europe.

There are 2 basic types of ocean currents—surface currents and deep water currents. Surface currents are usually wind driven and move in large, roughly circular patterns. These patterns are known as *gyres*. There are 2 main gyres in the Northern Hemisphere and 3 primary gyres in the Southern Hemisphere. Most surface currents are more than 50 miles wide and flow at speeds of about 136 miles per day.

The water temperature of surface currents may range from a low of 30°F to a high of 86°F. Surface currents are significant because they help regulate the water temperature throughout the world. They distribute the sun's heat to distant locations so that the tropics do not get too hot and the polar regions too cold. In other words, currents affect the earth's climate by driving warm water from the equator and cold water from the polar regions around the world.

Most surface currents are composed of warm water. Warm water tends to stay on top of colder water simply because it is lighter and less dense than cold water. As a result, warm-water currents flow over the top of deep-water or cold-water currents.

Current Events

Ocean currents can be either warm-water currents or cold-water currents. This activity will help you understand warm-water currents.

You'll need:
>
> a deep glass bowl
> red food coloring
> cold water
> a saucepan
> very hot (not boiling) water

What to do:
1. Fill the glass bowl about half full with cold tap water.
2. Fill the saucepan with water and heat on stove, but do not boil. Put several drops (5–10) of red food coloring into the hot water and mix thoroughly.
3. Slowly pour some of the hot water into the bowl of cold water.

What happens:

You will notice that the colored hot water stays on top of the cold water (after a while the hot water will begin to cool and eventually mix with the cooler water in the bowl). The hot water stays on top of the cool water because water expands when it is heated (ocean water is heated by the warmth of the sun). As the water expands it gets lighter, so it floats on top of the heavier, denser cold water.

Warm ocean currents usually begin around the warmest regions of the world (typically near the equator) and move across the ocean near the surface. Cold currents, on the other hand, usually begin in the polar regions as a result of melting ice. Because cold water is heavier than warm water, cold ocean currents flow at a greater depth.

Cold-water currents occur because of differences in the density of seawater. Colder and saltier water is denser than warm, less salty water—consequently it sinks to the bottom of the ocean. At the ice shelves in the polar regions of the world, the water is very cold and is weighted down with lots of salts. As that water sinks, warmer, less dense water rushes in to replace it closer to the surface. This action is known as *thermohaline* and occurs primarily in the North Atlantic and Antarctic regions. The sinking motion of the heavy water causes a current to form, which spreads out toward the equator. Typically, cold-water currents move much more slowly than warm-water currents.

Constantly changing … constantly moving … constantly building up and tearing down—that's the ocean. The incredible forces that sweep across the surface of the ocean and that are created by the oceans are all part of the daily "operations" of our planet. In many ways oceans regulate a great deal of what we do every day—things that we often take for granted.

So far you've discovered much about the marvels and mysteries of the ocean. In the next chapter, you'll be able to take a visit to a miniature ocean that might be in your own neighborhood or just down the road.

6 Visiting an Aquarium

A large group of jellyfish gently floats across the surface of the water. A great white shark slowly cruises in ever-decreasing circles looking for its next meal. A giant octopus is frightened, changes its color, and darts under a stony outcropping. Oversize green sea anemones crowd a shoreline waving their menacing tentacles in the surging water. The suction-cup arms of a starfish (sea star) cling tightly to a slippery rock.

Where is this place? It's not some distant shoreline or far away ocean. In fact, it may be just around the corner, down the highway, or a short vacation away. It's an aquarium—a place where hundreds of varieties of sea life and ocean-dwelling organisms are gathered for people to observe. Aquariums can be found in almost every state, from those that fringe the Pacific and Atlantic Oceans to those far inland on the plains and mountains of middle America.

A visit to an aquarium can be a magical and marvelous experience. Everything you have been learning in this book will come to life as you tour the numerous exhibits and observe the incredible array of sea plants and animal life. Hundreds of marine species, rolling waves, rocky pools, magnificent exhibits, and dozens of hands-on experiences with plants and animals of every size, shape, and description are some of the highlights that aquariums have to offer. Crashing surf, deep-ocean waters, and eye-popping exhibits provide you with rare opportunities to come face-to-face with a host of ocean creatures. Aquariums are places of wonder—where you can stroll, meander, skip, or dart from beach to ocean and back again all at your own pace. Even if you never have an opportunity to visit a real ocean or take a trip to the seashore, you will definitely want to plan a visit or vacation to a nearby aquarium.

Here's a list of some selected aquariums around the country. If you're not able to visit these aquariums in person, you may want to contact them by mail to request their literature or informational brochures. Several aquariums have their

own websites, which provide numerous opportunities to take an arm-chair journey through their exhibits and displays.

Aquarium Center
Iowa State Fairgrounds
3000 East Grand Avenue
Des Moines, IA 50317
(515) 263-0612
http://www.iowaaquarium.org

Birch Aquarium at Scripps
9500 Gilman Drive
La Jolla, CA 92093
(619) 534-3474
http://aqua.ucsd.edu/SBAM2/sbam_OOO.html

Cabrillo Marine Aquarium
3720 Stephen White Drive
San Pedro, CA 90732
(310) 548-7562
http://cyberfair.gsn.org/dodson/aquarium.html

The Florida Aquarium
701 Channelside Drive
Tampa, FL 33602
(813) 273-4000
http://www.sptimes.com/aquarium/default.html

John Shedd Aquarium
1200 South Lake Shore Drive
Chicago, IL 60605
(312) 939-2438
http://www.sheddnet.org

Mid-America Aqua Center
416 Hanley Industrial Court
Brentwood, MO 63144
(314) 647-9594
http://www.i-base.com/aquacntr/

Monterey Bay Aquarium
886 Cannery Row
Monterey, CA 93940
(800) 840-4880
http://www.mbayaq.org

National Aquarium in Baltimore
Pier 3, 501 East Pratt Street
Baltimore, MD 21202
(410) 659-4230
http://aqua.org

New England Aquarium
Central Wharf
Boston, MA 02110
(617) 973-5200
http://www.neaq.org

North Carolina Aquarium on Roanoke Island
P.O. Box 967
Manteo, NC 27954
(919) 473-3494
http://www.outer-banks.com/aqua.html

Oregon Coast Aquarium
2820 S.E. Ferry Slip Road
Newport, OR 97365
(541) 867-3474
http://www.aquarium.org

The Seattle Aquarium
1424 Fourth Avenue
Seattle, WA 98101
(206) 682-3474
http://seattleaquarium.org

Sea World of California
1720 South Shores Road
San Diego, CA 92109
(619) 226-3834
http://www.4adventure.com/seaworld/sw_california/frame.html

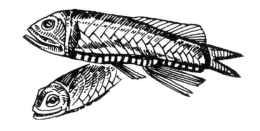

Sea World of Florida
7007 Sea World Drive
Orlando, FL 32821
(407) 363-2380
http://www.4adventure.com/seaworld/sw_florida/frame.html

Sea World of Ohio
1100 Sea World Drive
Aurora, OH 44202
(216) 562-8101
http://www.4adventure.com/seaworld/sw_ohio/frame.html

Sea World of Texas
10500 Sea World Drive
San Antonio, TX 78251
(210) 523-3606
http://www.4adventure.com/seaworld/sw_texas/frame.html

South Carolina Aquarium
57 Hasell Street
Charleston, SC 29401
(803) 720-1990
http://www.awod.com/scaquarium/

Steinhart Aquarium
California Academy of Sciences
Golden Gate Park
San Francisco, CA 94118
(415) 750-7145
http://www.calacademy.org/aquarium/

Tennessee Aquarium
One Broad Street
Chattanooga, TN 37401
(800) 262-0695
http://www.tennis.org

Virginia Marine Science Museum
717 General Booth Boulevard
Virginia Beach, VA 23451
(757) 425-FISH
http://www.whro.org/vmsm/

The Waikiki Aquarium
2777 Kalakaua Avenue
Honolulu, HI 96815
(808) 923-9741
http://www.mic.hawaii.edu/aquarium/

Aquariums are as varied and different as the creatures that inhabit them. Some aquariums are enormous, spreading over several acres of lands, while other aquariums are smaller with only a few rooms and a couple of tide pools. Actually, no two aquariums are the same, but they all share one vital function: to provide a marine science exhibition facility for public education and oceanic research. A primary goal of any aquarium is to help the public better understand and preserve the natural resources of seashores and oceans locally and around the world.

Parts of an Aquarium

Although each aquarium has different displays and exhibits, in general, aquariums are divided into several major sections. These different areas allow the aquarium to feature organisms that are related or those that inhabit a similar ecosystem. Many aquariums present special displays about marine life in the local area. Let's take a stroll through some of the sections you might find in a typical aquarium.

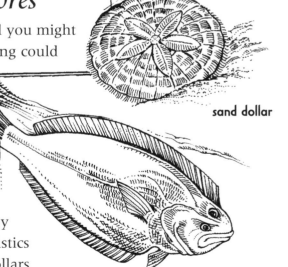

black skimmer

sand dollar

flounder (halibut)

Sandy Shores

One look at a long stretch of sandy beach and you might think that it was a quiet deserted area. Nothing could be further from the truth. Many creatures lie hidden beneath the sand—clams, snails, fleas, shrimp—while others are carefully camouflaged to blend in with the natural colors of the sand. Shore birds, fishes, and other predators come and go with the tides to prey on clams and worms beneath the sand.

In this section of the aquarium you may discover displays that replicate the characteristics and conditions of shore life. Magical sand dollars lie half-buried in sandy areas with a steady current tilted up like wheels, broadside to the current, in order to capture food particles sweeping by. However, because of their small size, sand dollars risk getting washed away or knocked flat by large waves. To stabilize themselves, these creatures swallow grains of sand for ballast, giving them additional weight and balance.

You may also find flat fish that start their lives just like any other fish, swimming upright with an eye on each side of their heads and color on both sides of their bodies. But as the fish gets older one eye begins to shift and move toward the other, and the fish begins to lean sideways as it swims. By the time the young fish settles on the bottom, its transformation is complete: both eyes have moved to one side of its head, and it swims horizontally. The eyed side is colored to match the colors of the sand and the blind side turns ivory or pure white. Interestingly, some species of flat fish have their eyes on the left side of their heads, and some species have their eyes on the right side of their heads. Then, there are some species that can be either left-eyed or right-eyed.

Tide Pools

Life in a tide pool can be turbulent and harsh. As you have learned earlier in this book, tide pools are home to some of the ocean's most incredible creatures. Not only must animals be able to hold fast to the slippery rocks and endure the constant bashing of waves, they must also be able to locate enough food *and* keep away from any predators. A few of the many organisms found in the ocean's tide pools are listed below:

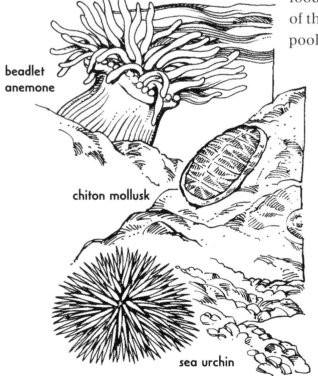

beadlet anemone

chiton mollusk

sea urchin

PLANTS	ANIMALS
algae	anemones
kelp	barnacles
plankton	crabs
rockweed	fish
sea lettuce	mussels
seaweed	sea stars (starfish)
surf grass	snails

Contrary to popular belief, most of the sea foam you see in tide pools is not the result of pollution. Strong fall and winter waves crush algae and seaweeds, which release proteins, sugars, fats, and bits of plant debris. These materials then float on the surface and are whipped into a froth, or foam, by the rough seas, which in turn floats into shore causing the beach to look like a giant bubble bath.

Coastal Waters

This section focuses on those creatures that live offshore, the ones that provide us with a significant part of our diet as well as those that migrate great distances through the ocean. Sharks, tuna, salmon, and whales are just a few of the many animals you'll discover here.

In the coastal waters you may discover a smack (a group) of jellyfish. Interestingly, jellyfish float through life with no brain, no spine, no bones, and no heart. In fact, these animals are more than 95 percent water. They swim by gently contracting a band of muscle fibers that encircles the bell-shaped part of its body. Tentacles covered with stinging cells trail from the jelly's body. Fish unlucky enough to swim into these tentacles are stung so much that they eventually die. The tentacles of some species may be as long as 100 feet. In Japan, jellyfish are considered a delicacy and dried jelly's are sold in many stores.

albacore tuna

moon jellyfish

humpback whale

Coral Reef

Coral reefs are found in many tropical parts of oceans around the world. Each reef is composed of the skeletons of tiny animals known as polyps. Polyps have soft bodies and mouths that are ringed by stinging tentacles. The polyps build skeletons of limestone around themselves. As they die they leave their skeletons behind. These skeletons fuse together to make a coral reef. The upper layer of a reef is made of living corals, which build upon the skeletons of millions and millions of dead polyps.

Coral reefs are also home to an incredible array of plants and animals. Thousands of tropical fish; dozens of species of sponges, algae, and seaweed; and dozens of marine organisms from the smallest shrimp to the largest sharks may inhabit a

coral reef. Warm waters and lots of available food make a coral reef an ideal habitat for many underwater creatures. They are also popular for scuba divers and snorklers to examine the rich bounty of the world's oceans.

Fantastic Fact

The Great Barrier Reef off the coast of Australia is 1,200 miles long. It is the largest structure in the world made by living organisms.

In this part of the aquarium you can examine some of the many inhabitants of coral reefs. One of those inhabitants may be brine shrimp. Brine shrimp are a common organism around many coral reefs. Here's how you can grow some at home.

 ## See the Sea Shrimp

You'll need:

> brine shrimp eggs (available from any pet store)
> noniodized or kosher salt (available at most grocery stores)
> 2-quart pot
> water
> teaspoon
> medicine dropper
> hand lens or inexpensive microscope
> aged tap water (see below)

What to do:

1. Fill the pot with 2 quarts of water and allow it to sit for 3 days, stirring it occasionally. (Most city water has chlorine in it, which will kill the shrimp. By letting it "age" for several days the chlorine gas can escape from the water.)
2. Mix 5 teaspoons of noniodized salt with the water until dissolved.
3. Add $1/2$ teaspoon of brine shrimp eggs to the salt water and place the pot in a warm spot.
4. Use the medicine dropper to remove some eggs from the water and observe them with your hand lens or microscope. Check a drop of water every day. You may wish to create a series of drawings or illustrations to record the growth of your brine shrimp.

What happens:

The brine shrimp eggs will begin to hatch in about 2 days. They will continue to grow in the water until they reach their adult stage. You will be able to watch this growth process over a period of many days.

Brine shrimp eggs that are purchased at a pet store are the fertilized eggs of very tiny animals called brine shrimp. The eggs you purchase are dried and can be kept for very long periods of time (especially when kept in a dry place). When they are added to the salt water, the eggs "wake up" and begin to grow. Although they are very small, you can watch them grow for many days. *Note:* Brine shrimp eggs are sold as fish food for aquariums.

Wetlands Exhibit

Wetlands are magnificent and diverse environments. They are home to an incredible variety of plant and animal life, some of which is found nowhere else on the planet. Scientists have estimated that more than 5,000 different kinds of vegetation grow in wetlands and that nearly half of all the animal species in the world inhabit wetland areas.

Wetlands are defined as a mingling of water and land. The water may be standing (as in a shallow pond or quiet marsh), or it may be slowly flowing (e.g., the Everglades in Florida or along a seacoast). The water may be a few inches or up to several feet deep. Wetlands occur along the shores of rivers, streams, lakes, ponds, coastal regions, and other low-lying areas. Most of the oceanic wetlands in the United States are located in the Southeast, the Gulf Coast, and the northeastern coastal states. Smaller numbers of coastal wetlands are found in western states. It is estimated that there are currently 95 million acres of wetlands in this country.

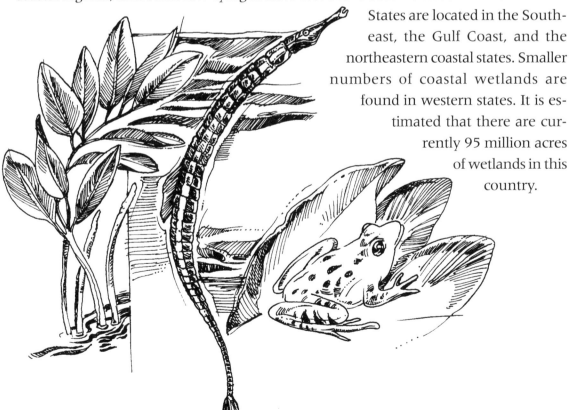

Although most people think that wetlands are nothing more than swampy areas crawling with snakes and crocodiles and buzzing with swarms of mosquitoes, these ecosystems are extremely important to the life and survival of oceans. If it were not for wetlands, many plants and animals (including humans) would not be able to survive.

- Wetlands are major breeding grounds for several different kinds of animals. Many species need the seclusion and safety of these areas in order to reproduce and raise their young.
- Wetlands control excessive flooding. The spongy thick vegetation of wetland areas helps absorb rainwater and slows the excess flow of rivers.
- Wetlands are also water purification areas. Wetlands vegetation can filter and absorb wastes, pollution, and contamination from streams and rivers, thus ensuring a clean water supply for living organisms.
- Wetlands protect and shelter a wide variety of wildlife. These sanctuaries ensure the protection of many species including pipefish, ghost shrimp, pricklebacks, rockfish, and flatfish. Some can live nowhere else on the planet. When wetlands are filled in or destroyed, these creatures may become extinct.

This section of an aquarium offers visitors a unique glimpse into this special ecosystem. The relationship between coastal wetlands and the health and viability of coastal areas is an area rich with discoveries.

 # Small to Big

The animals at an aquarium come in all sizes and shapes. Here's how you can learn about the relative sizes of some of those creatures.

You'll need:

A skein of yarn (available at any hobby or fabric store)
scissors
index cards
markers
the chart below
a large open area (living room, backyard, driveway)

What to do:

1. Use the chart below to cut the yarn into different lengths.
2. Lay each length of yarn on the floor or ground.

3. At the end of each length of yarn place an index card on which you have written the corresponding animal's name.

Hermit crab—$^1/_2$ inch
Harbor seal—6 feet
Sea urchin—4 inches
Leopard shark—6 feet
Kelp crab—4 inches
Ochre sea star—12 inches
Sea lion (adult)—$10^1/_2$ feet
Puffin (wing span)—36 inches
Giant octopus—27 feet
Sunflower star—52 inches (arm span)
Sea otter—58 inches
Killer whale—27 feet
Gray whale—39 feet
Porpoise—6 feet
Whale shark—49 feet
Humpback whale—52 feet
Sperm whale—60 feet
Your height—_____ feet

(All measurements provided courtesy of the Oregon Coast Aquarium.)

What happens:

You'll notice that marine animals come in a wide variety of lengths. Some are very short; others are very long. This activity will allow you to compare the lengths of selected animals frequently found in an aquarium. You may want to do some additional reading on some of these creatures (a list of selected books is provided in chapter 9) to learn about where each animal lives, what and how it eats, behavior patterns, natural enemies, and other interesting information.

Other Possible Exhibits

Each aquarium has a different focus or emphasis depending on where it is located. For example, aquariums in Florida and Louisiana may emphasize sea life in mangrove swamps and sawgrass marshes; aquariums in California and Hawaii may have numerous exhibits on tide pools and whales; and midwestern aquariums may emphasize freshwater fish or other aquatic organisms. It's safe to say that no two aquariums are the same; each is unique.

Depending on where you live or what aquariums you may visit, you will discover a host of fascinating exhibits awaiting your discovery. The list below details a few displays that may be found in a public aquarium.

SEABIRD AVIARY

An open-air, walk-through aviary (large bird cage) allows visitors to see several species of seabirds up close. Tufted puffins, auklets, guillemots, murres, and oystercatchers may be part of this unique bird collection.

SEA OTTER EXHIBIT

Sea otters are always a delight to watch. One can spend hours watching them swim through tunnels, nooks, and crannies. At some aquariums, visitors have several vantage points from which they can observe the otters above and below the water surface.

SEAL AND SEA LION EXHIBIT

The seal and sea lion pools are yet another popular section of an aquarium. Rocky pools, a short beach, and several rocky islands simulate the natural environment in which these creatures live in the wild.

rhinoceros auklet

puffin

ancient murrelet

KELP FOREST

Kelp forests look like enormous underwater jungles. Here you will discover an amazing collection of plant life and an equally amazing collection of ocean life that live in and among these incredible plants.

SEA TURTLE EXHIBIT

Sea turtles can be found around the world. Some species are on the endangered species list and need to be protected. This exhibit provides you with wonderful information about the lives of sea turtles and how they can be protected.

FROGS, TOADS, AND SALAMANDERS

This exhibit may be an interactive introduction to these delightful amphibians. You can discover information about their diversity, behavior, adaptations, and conservation.

WHALE TANK

In this exhibit visitors may be able to observe one or more whale species. You'll also learn some incredible information about whales around the world.

Aquariums provide us with opportunities to examine, explore, and learn about the discoveries made by working scientists around the world. They also allow us to make our own discoveries about the wonderful world of oceans near and far. Aquariums are magical places that invite questions, provide answers, and stimulate numerous investigations about life in this watery environment. Plan to visit one in person or via the Internet and learn more about oceans and their inhabitants.

mother seal and pup

sea lion

7 ⟫ A Part of Your Life

The food you eat, the medicines you take, the weather you enjoy, the products you use, the animals you learn about—all these items (and many more) are part of your everyday life. Many of these items come from, or are influenced by, the oceans of the world. In fact, the world's oceans probably have more to do with your daily life than you originally thought.

It doesn't make any difference where you are. You may live high in the mountains of Colorado, far out on the plains of Nebraska, deep in the Arizona desert, along the streets of Chicago, or among the lakes of Minnesota. No matter where you live or what you do, your daily life is dependent upon or influenced by oceans. It's amazing to think so much of our everyday lives includes something related to the oceans. And many scientists speculate that our lives in the future will be influenced even more by the world's oceans. Let's take a look at some of the many ways oceans touch our lives.

Food Resources

- In 1993, 98 million tons of fish came from oceans—70 percent of it for human consumption.
- Only about 300 of the world's 20,000 species of fish are caught for commercial purposes.
- World consumption of seafood exceeds that of either pork or beef.
- In 1993 the U.S. commercial catch of fish and shellfish was worth almost $3.7 billion.
- An estimated 200 million people worldwide depend on fishing for their livelihood.

Mineral Resources

- If mined, the gold suspended in seawater would yield 9 pounds per person.
- There are more minerals—from arsenic to zinc—in the world's oceans than in any other place.

Other Products

- Many different types of algae are used in Japanese-style cooking.
- Seaweed contains an ingredient—*carrageenan*—which is used in the manufacturing of ice cream.
- Oyster shells are included in natural calcium supplements.
- Cod liver oil comes from the Norwegian cod.

Shipping

- 80 percent of the world's trade is carried by ships.
- In 1990 there were 78,336 ships that could each carry at least 10,000 cubic feet of cargo.

Recreation

- In 1991, 8.9 million saltwater anglers spent about $5 billion on travel and equipment.
- Scuba diving is a worldwide industry worth about $2.5 billion each year.

Aquaculture

- Fish farming produces more than 12 million tons of fish each year.

Nonrenewable Resources

- 27 percent of the U.S. production of natural gas comes from offshore drilling.
- 13 percent of the U.S. production of oil comes from offshore drilling.

Pollution

- More than half of the ocean pollution worldwide comes from runoff and land-based discharges.

Medicines

Many chemists, biologists, and other scientists believe that the oceans of the world are a "gold mine" of potentially new and exciting medicines. Many of the medicines that we use every day come from terrestrial (land-based) plants and animals. But scientists are continuing to search for more effective drugs for selected diseases, more powerful drugs for specific illnesses, and new drugs to combat new strains of germs and bacteria. Two of the most feared diseases in the world—AIDS and cancer—are propelling scientists to look for new and vigorous medicines that can cure or even wipe out these afflictions.

Recently, scientists have been making some startling discoveries about medicines and drugs that originate in the ocean. The prospects for medical breakthroughs are enormous and are made possible because marine organisms have evolved different survival techniques than have terrestrial plants and animals. They are able to ward off diseases and infections with substances much different than current drugs. They are able to create enzymes and antibodies more efficiently than land creatures. They also have different means of converting sunlight into chemical energy.

What this means is some exciting new advances in medical technology. Let's take a look at a few:

- Scientists in Japan have discovered that stock left over from processing scallops contains an anticancer agent.
- A substance obtained from sponges—*manoalide*—is being tested as an anti-inflammatory drug.
- A substance in shark cartilage has been shown to restrict the growth of body tumors.
- A group of enzymes, known as omega III fatty acids, which come from certain fish and marine mammals, reduces the build-up of cholesterol in the blood.
- A specific drug—*halenguinone*—has been extracted from sponges and used as a powerful new antibiotic.
- Another drug—*didemnin*—obtained from tunicates (also known as sea squirts) has been extremely effective in treating certain types of cancer.
- Scientists have known about a substance in the shells of crabs, lobsters, and shrimp known as *chitin*. Recently, however, this substance has been used in a wide variety of medical applications such as sutures, bandages, burn dressings, drug delivery systems, food additives, and dietary supplements.
- *Alginic acid*, which comes from a certain species of seaweed, is being used to treat diabetics.

It is obvious that the world's oceans may also be the world's "medicine cabinet," as the potential for new discoveries is enormous. New drugs and medicines are being discovered at an increasingly rapid rate. Indeed, we may soon find that many or most of the medicines we take to fight illnesses and many of the drugs that are prescribed to combat diseases may originate in the depths of the oceans. You may want to ask your family doctor about some of the medicines she or he prescribes that have their origins in the ocean. You may be surprised at the response.

Food

If you go to a large grocery store, you might be amazed at the enormous variety of foods that are available from every corner of the world and from thousands and thousands of manufacturers. A modern-day supermarket is a splash of colors, a feast for the eyes, and a panorama of enticing sights and smells. Every type of food and food product can be found in most grocery stores.

You may not think much about the foods your parents or guardians bring home and cook for dinner, but you have undoubtedly had some type of seafood or fish product recently. In fact, it's amazing to think about the incredible variety of fish that is available in most stores—fish that is as fresh as the previous day and fish that has been frozen and shipped halfway around the world. You may have had a dinner at home or eaten a meal in a restaurant that came from several different locations throughout North America or from a host of countries throughout the world.

 ## From Sea to Shining Sea

Visit a local grocery store and take along a list similar to the one following. This list represents several varieties of fish that are commonly found in most supermarkets throughout North America and that are sold as food. Check off each type of fish as you locate it in the store. You may want to visit the fresh fish department, the frozen fish section, and the canned food section. How many of the following are in your local supermarket?

anchovies	catfish	clams
cod	crab	flounder
grouper	haddock	halibut
herring	lobster	mackerel
monkfish	mussels	octopus
orange roughy	oysters	perch
pollock	salmon	sardines
scallops	scrod	shrimp
swordfish	tuna	whitefish
whiting		

You may also want to obtain some of the varieties of fish above and prepare a seafood meal or two for members of your family. Here are some seafood recipes that I think you'll enjoy preparing and, most of all, will also enjoy eating.

Note: Some of these recipes require the use of a stove, hot oven, or cooking oil. Please invite an adult to help you prepare these dishes.

 # Salmon Burgers

You'll need:

2 slices of bread
1 14-ounce can of salmon (drained)
1 large egg
2 tablespoons teriyaki sauce
hamburger buns

What to do:

1. In a large bowl mix together the can of salmon with the large egg (use your hands to thoroughly mix the ingredients).
2. Tear the two slices of bread into very small pieces. Measure a $^1/_2$ cup of crumbs and mix them into the salmon mixture.
3. Add teriyaki sauce to the bowl and mix into the salmon.
4. Shape the salmon mixture into 4, 3-inch round patties and place on waxed paper.
5. In a nonstick frying pan, cook the patties for about 10 minutes over medium heat, flipping once, until golden brown and cooked through.
6. Serve the patties on hamburger buns.

 # Fish Soup

You'll need:

4 carrots
1 onion
1 celery stalk
1 tablespoon vegetable oil
1 pound small red potatoes, cut into small cubes
2 8-ounce bottles of clam juice
1 10-ounce can of whole baby clams
1 extra large vegetable bouillon cube
1 pound of cod fillet
1 large tomato

What to do:

1. **Note: Have an adult help.** Slice the carrots, onion, and celery into small pieces. Put them into a 5-quart dutch oven or large saucepan with the vegetable oil.

2. Cook the vegetables over medium heat until they are lightly browned.

3. Add 2 cups of water, the potatoes, clam juice, clams (with their liquid), and bouillon. Heat to boiling over high heat. Cover and simmer for 7 to 10 minutes until the potatoes are almost tender.

4. While the pot is simmering, cut the cod into 2-inch chunks. Cut the tomato into 1-inch chunks.

5. Stir the cod and tomato chunks into the soup. Turn the heat to high and heat to boiling. Reduce the heat to low and simmer until the fish flakes easily when tested with a fork. Serves 4.

 # Crab Cakes

You'll need:

1 pound of crabmeat

1 cup of bread crumbs

1 egg, beaten

1 tablespoon mayonnaise

1 teaspoon Dijon mustard

1 teaspoon Worcestershire sauce

salt and pepper to taste

What to do:

1. Combine all the ingredients in a large bowl.

2. On a sheet of waxed paper, form into 6 patties.

3. Fry the patties in a small amount of cooking oil until they are golden brown. Turn once.

4. Serve plain or on hamburger rolls.

8 Oceans in Danger

For hundreds of years people thoughtlessly dumped their trash, garbage, and pollutants into the world's oceans. It was mistakenly thought that the oceans were large enough to hold vast amounts of waste or that the salinity (salt content) of the water was great enough to kill dangerous bacteria or germs.

Unfortunately, we now know that pollution of the oceans is a serious problem in many parts of the world. Every year vast amounts of industrial waste, sewage, plastics, oil, and radioactive waste are dumped into the sea. The results can not only be startling, but dangerous as well. Here are some examples:

Oil Spills

If an oil tanker runs aground or crashes into the shoreline huge amounts of oil can leak into the sea. The oil spreads across the surface of the water forming a slick that can be carried ashore by ocean currents or winds. There the oil kills seabirds, poisons shellfish and other edible sea life, and endangers mammals and other creatures that live near the shore.

In March 1989 the oil tanker *Exxon Valdez* ran aground off the coast of Alaska. The ship leaked more than 12 million gallons of oil into the water. The oil quickly spread up and down the Alaskan coast killing nearly 100,000 sea birds (including 150 rare bald eagles), 1,000 sea otters, and hundreds of thousands of fish, seals, and shellfish.

Sea of Oil

The following activity will help you understand what happens to a seabird that gets oil on its feathers.

You'll need:

> 2 cereal bowls
> vegetable oil
> water
> 2 feathers (available at any craft or hobby store)

Note: Don't use a bird feather found outside. It may contain germs or organisms that could be harmful to your health.

What to do:

1. Fill each bowl about half full with water.
2. Put about 1 tablespoon of vegetable oil onto the surface of the water in one of the bowls.
3. Lay one of the feathers on the surface of the water in the bowl without the oil.
4. Remove that feather and blow on it. Also, stroke it between your fingers. Notice how that feather reacts when you blow on it and when you touch it.
5. Place the other feather in the bowl with the vegetable oil.
6. Remove that feather and blow on it. Also, stroke it between your fingers. Notice how it reacts.

What happens:

The feather that you put into the bowl of water does not get soaked and is light enough to be moved by your breath. The feather that was placed in the bowl of water with oil appears to be soaked and is coated with a layer of oil. It does not move very much when you blow on it.

Birds' feathers are designed to repel water. By keeping water away from their skin, birds are able to conserve heat and stay warm. When their feathers become coated with oil they lose this ability. The fibers of oil-covered feathers tend to stick together. As a result, they stick to the skin of a bird, thus preventing it from conserving heat. Also, oil on their feathers tends to add so much weight that many birds are unable to fly, particularly young ones, so they may be unable to obtain their food or they may become an easy prey for other animals.

 # Clean It Up!

Cleaning up an oil spill is not as easy as it looks. This activity will give you a chance to try out several different methods.

You'll need:

> water
> vegetable oil
> large plastic tub
> test materials: paper towels, Styrofoam "peanuts," aquarium net, drinking straw, dish detergent, string, straw, sand, diatomous earth

What to do:

1. Fill the large plastic tub half-way with water.
2. Pour a cup of vegetable oil on the surface of the water.
3. Use each of the following materials (one at a time) to see how well it cleans up the oil spill (you may need to add additional vegetable oil after each time).
   a. paper towel—put it on the oil and remove it
   b. Styrofoam "peanuts" (used as packing material)—place on the oil and remove after several minutes
   c. aquarium net—try to scoop the oil into the net for disposal
   d. drinking straw—put the straw in the water and blow a ring of bubbles around the oil spill (the bubbles will contain the spill)
   e. dish detergent—put several drops directly on the spill and try to disperse the oil
   f. string—float a piece of string on the water and encircle the oil. Try to move the oil slick from one side of the tub to the other.
   g. straw—place pieces of straw on the surface of the oil to soak it up
   h. sand—sprinkle some playground sand on the surface of the oil and note what happens
   i. diatomous earth, also known as kaolin (available at most garden shops)—sprinkle some on the surface of the oil and note the effects.
4. Note which method or combination of methods works best in cleaning up the oil spill.
5. You may wish to repeat this activity, except have a partner make waves or ripples on the surface of the water as you try to clean up the oil spill.

What happens:

There are many different methods and materials that can be used to clean up an oil spill depending on the conditions of the sea, the weather at the time of the cleanup, the extent of the oil spill, and the people and resources that are available. Most methods involve containment of the spill, absorption of the oil, skimming the oil off the surface, coagulating the oil so it can be gathered, and sinking the oil to the ocean bottom. Each method has its advantages and disadvantages and this activity will help you learn about some of the problems associated with oil spill clean-ups.

Sewage Dumping

In many places around the world, untreated sewage is dumped directly into the ocean. Not only does this make the ocean unsafe to swim in due to the millions of dangerous bacteria and other organisms that can infect humans, it also depletes the water of necessary oxygen. When large quantities of sewage are placed in the water, it stimulates the growth of algae. Sewage contains nutrients that algae need to grow. But when there are too many nutrients, then too much algae grows. And eventually when algae begins to die it uses up extra supplies of oxygen in the water. The result is less oxygen available for other marine organisms, including plants and animals. As a result, these organisms suffocate or die from a severe lack of oxygen.

Garbage

Imagine if your house was filled to the brim with thousands upon thousands of pounds of garbage. (You might want to read the poem "Sarah Cynthia Sylvia Stout Would Not Take the Garbage Out" in *Where the Sidewalk Ends* by Shel Silverstein, New York: HarperCollins, 1974.) Imagine trying to live in that kind of environment. How would you get around? How would you breathe? And simply, how would you survive for very long?

Now imagine the same thing happening in the ocean or a certain spot in the ocean. Imagine tin cans, glass bottles, metal drums, plastic items of every shape and description, paper products, wire, wood, decayed and spoiled food, and every other type of garbage item being dumped into the ocean on a regular basis. Well, you don't have to imagine it, because it's happening each and every day and each and every year.

- Each year ships at sea dump approximately 6 million tons of garbage into the ocean. Many of the items dumped into the sea are nonbiodegradable, which means that they do not break down, decay, or rot for many years.

As a result, thousands of ocean animals get trapped or entangled in these items and eventually die.

- Young seals and sea lions, shorebirds, and other creatures become entangled in the plastic rings used to hold 6-packs of soda. They eventually strangle themselves to death.
- Whales, porpoises, and dolphins ingest plastic bags, which block their stomachs, causing them to starve to death.
- Fish and other sea creatures become caught in old nets, tin cans, and bottles. Unable to swim, they cannot seek food and eventually die of starvation.
- Seabirds eat small plastic items floating in the water. The items get caught in their throats and they die.
- Bottom-feeding fish eat cigarette butts, metal pop tops, and paper items which clog their digestive systems.

Industrial Pollution

Many of the world's factories and industries are located near the coastlines of oceans or along rivers that feed into oceans. It is not uncommon for these industries to discharge enormous amounts of chemical wastes into the water. These wastes may include such dangerous poisons and pollutants as mercury, cadmium, lead, tin, and copper. Often, these chemicals become concentrated in a certain area (due to tides and ocean currents) and kill fish and other animals that feed upon those fish.

- In the 1950s it was not unusual for many factories in Japan to discharge large amounts of mercury into offshore waters. Over time, this mercury was ingested by fish and eventually built up to highly concentrated levels. When people ate this fish, they got highly concentrated doses of mercury. In 1952 more than 100 people died and more than 2,000 were paralyzed as a result of eating shellfish and fish contaminated by the mercury.

 ## Plenty of Pollution

Ocean pollution can take many forms. Some of it we can see, but many types cannot be seen but are just as dangerous. Although this experiment uses fresh water, the results are just as dramatic.

You'll need:

    4 small glass jars without lids (baby food jars work well)
    aged water (fill a large container with tap water and allow to sit

uncovered for 3 days so that the chlorine gas that is present in most city water supplies is allowed to escape into the atmosphere)

pond soil and pond water **(Note: These two items may not be available in some areas of the country.)**

liquid plant fertilizer

liquid dish detergent

motor oil

vinegar

What to do:

1. Label each of the 4 jars as follows: "A," "B," "C," and "D."
2. For each of the 4 jars do the following: fill each half full with aged tap water, put in a $1/2$ inch of pond soil, add 1 teaspoon of plant fertilizer, then fill each jar with pond water and algae to within 1 inch from the top.
3. Allow the jars to sit in a sunny location (a window sill) for 2 weeks.
4. Then add the following to each jar separately: In Jar "A" add 2 tablespoons of liquid detergent; in Jar "B" add enough motor oil to cover the surface; in Jar "C" add a $1/2$ cup of vinegar; and leave Jar "D" as it is.
5. Allow the jars to sit for an additional 4 weeks.

What happens:

You'll note that the growth that took place during the first 2 weeks of this experiment has been severely changed with the addition of the detergent, motor oil, and vinegar in jars A, B, and C. In fact, those jars may indicate little or no growth taking place, while the organisms in jar D continue to grow.

Detergent, motor oil, and vinegar are pollutants that prevent the organisms in the first 3 jars from obtaining the nutrients and oxygen they need to continue growing. The detergent shows what happens when large quantities of soap are released into the ocean; the motor oil shows what happens to organisms after an oil spill; and the vinegar shows what can happen when high levels of acids are added to the ocean. When industries, factories, and homeowners put these kinds of pollutants into streams, rivers, and other water sources, they eventually wash into the ocean—resulting in serious effects on deep sea plants and animals.

Agricultural Chemicals

Populations of people are increasing in many countries around the world—particularly in underdeveloped countries. To help feed all these people, farmers need to grow more and more food. In order to do this they often spray larger and larger amounts of pesticides (chemicals that kill harmful pests), insecticides (chemicals

that kill insects), and fertilizers (chemicals that stimulate the growth of plants) on their crops. Ideally, harmful pests are killed off and bigger harvests are ensured with the application of these chemicals.

But it's important to note that about one-half of all the chemicals put on fields and other growing areas get washed away by rains and floods. These chemicals eventually make their way into streams and rivers. Then they are carried downriver and into the sea. The results can be devastating.

When fertilizers enter the ocean they tend to reduce the amount of oxygen in the water. As a result, fish, shellfish, and other animals cannot breathe and eventually die.

Nutrients Away

Agricultural chemicals in the soil often are washed into rivers and streams and eventually into the ocean. Here's an activity that demonstrates that process.

You'll need:

> 2 rectangular cake pans (9 x 13 inches)
> grass seed
> soil
> water
> red food coloring
> a brick or heavy book

What to do:

1. Fill both of the rectangular cake pans with soil. In each pan, sprinkle some grass seeds on the surface, then press into the soil. Water thoroughly. Put in a sunny place for about a week.

2. After the grass in both pans has reached a height of 2 to 3 inches, take the pans outdoors. Place one end of each pan on a book or brick so that the pans are at an angle.

3. Sprinkle about 40 to 50 drops of red food coloring onto the soil in one of the pans.

4. Fill a pitcher with water and pour it at the top of the first pan (the one without the food coloring). Let the water run through the soil and out the bottom. Note the color of the water.

5. Fill the pitcher again and pour it at the top of the second pan (the one with the red food coloring). Let the water run through the soil and out the bottom. Note the color of the water.

What happens:

The water that flows through the soil in the second pan will be red in color. Each time the experiment is repeated (with the same mixture of soil) the color will become progressively lighter. Eventually the water will run clean.

The red food coloring represents the chemicals that are artificially placed on or in the soil. These chemicals help plants grow and keep harmful pests away. However, whenever there is a lot of rain or water runoff the water takes these chemicals with it into a nearby water source. There the chemicals eventually run downriver and into the ocean. There they may be ingested by fish and other aquatic organisms, thus beginning their poisonous journey.

Overfishing

As the number of people in the world grows, so does the need for more food. Many people and many nations turn to the oceans as a ready source of food. Unfortunately, more and more fish are being taken from the ocean faster than they can reproduce and grow. As a result, entire populations of some species of fish are being seriously depleted and are in danger of becoming extinct.

Several nations have enacted bans on overfishing or have put limits on the number of any single species that can be taken in one year. Unfortunately, some of these laws or restrictions are difficult to enforce (the oceans are large and policing whole fleets of fishing vessels is almost impossible). While there are laws that protect many fish, these laws are often broken. The result is that some varieties of whales and several species of fish may be entirely wiped out in just a few years.

There's no question that the oceans of the world are in serious danger. It's not easy to erase hundreds of years of abuse. Many public policy organizations, environmental groups, concerned citizen associations, local governments, and individuals are working hard to reduce, slow down, or eliminate some of these problems. But creative solutions take time to plan and to implement.

9 What You Can Do

The oceans of the world are rich and valuable environments. But they are also in danger. Seas are being polluted by oil spills, indiscriminate dumping of trash and garbage, and a host of other human activities. Overfishing is severely reducing many species of marine life. Erosion and habitat disturbance are severely affecting seashores and the plants and animals that live there.

Many young people, such as yourself, are interested in preserving oceans around the world. By joining together we can all work toward saving these valuable ecosystems. Although many oceans are in critical or severe danger, there are things we can do today that will help preserve and protect the world's oceans for tomorrow as well as for many years in the future.

Contact Environmental Groups

There are many environmental groups throughout the United States working to save and protect the oceans of the world. These organizations not only produce films, brochures, and other types of information for the public, but they also raise money to help protect species of fish and marine animals, legislate for strict environmental laws, and provide opportunities for people to learn more about sea life.

Perhaps you and your friends and classmates can contact several of these groups and ask for information on the work they do and the types of printed materials they have available for students. Several of these organizations have local groups in cities all across the United States. You may wish to contact the leaders of one or more of these local affiliates and learn about some of the programs and information they provide. By joining with others in your community and throughout the country you can make a difference.

American Cetacean Society
P.O. Box 1391
San Pedro, CA 90733-0391
(310) 548-6279
Website: www.acsonline.org
An organization that works in the areas of conservation, education, and research to protect marine mammals, especially whales, dolphins, and porpoises and the oceans they live in.

American Littoral Society
Sandy Hook
Highlands, NJ 07732
(201) 291-0055
A national organization interested in the study and conservation of coastal habitats, barrier beaches, wetlands,
estuaries, and near-shore waters, and their fish,
shellfish, and mammal resources.

American Oceans Campaign
725 Arizona Avenue, Suite 102
Santa Monica, CA 90401
(310) 576-6162
Website: http://www.americanoceans.org
This organization is dedicated to the restoration and preservation of the world's coastal waters, estuaries, bays, wetlands, deep oceans, and their living resources.

Center for Marine Conservation
1725 DeSales Street NW, Suite 500
Washington, DC 20036
(202) 429-5609
This organization is dedicated to preserving marine wildlife and their habitats, and to conserving coastal and ocean resources.

Cetacean Society International
P.O. Box 953
Georgetown, CT 06829
(203) 544-8617
This group is dedicated to the protection of all cetaceans (whales, dolphins, and porpoises) and the marine environment on a global basis.

Coastal Conservation Association
4801 Woodway, Suite 220 West
Houston, TX 77056
(713) 626-4222
An organization organized for the purpose of promoting and advancing the preservation, conservation, and protection of the marine, animal, and plant life along the coastal areas of the United States.

The Coral Reef Alliance
809 Delaware Street
Berkeley, CA 94710
(510) 528-2492
Website: http://www.coral.org/
An organization that works to promote coral reef conservation around the world.

International Marine Mammal Project
Earth Island Institute
300 Broadway, Suite 28
San Francisco, CA 94133
(800)-DOLPHIN
This group is committed to ending dolphin mortality caused by the U.S. and international tuna industries, to stopping the use of drift nets, and to promoting sustainable fishing practices.

International Oceanographic Foundation
4600 Rickenbacker Causeway
Virginia Key
Miami, FL 33149
(305) 361-4888
This organization seeks to acquaint and educate the general public concerning the vital role of the oceans to all life on the planet.

International Wildlife Coalition (IWC) and The Whale Adoption Project
70 East Falmouth Highway
East Falmouth, MA 02536
(508) 548-8328
Website: http://www.webcom.com.iwcwww
The IWC is dedicated to preserving wildlife and their habitats. The Whale Adoption Project protects marine mammals.

Marine Environmental Research Institute
772 West End Avenue
New York, NY 10025
(212) 864-6285
This nonprofit organization is dedicated to protecting the health and biodiversity of the marine environment. Additionally, they address the problems of marine pollution, endangered species, and environmental emergencies affecting marine life.

Marine Technology Center
1828 L Street NW, Suite 906
Washington, DC 20036-5104
(202) 775-5966
An ocean-oriented professional society that encourages the development of technology and scientific principles necessary to work effectively in all ocean areas.

National Coalition for Marine Conservation
3 West Market Street
Leesburg, VA 20176
(703) 777-0037
A privately supported organization devoted exclusively to the conservation of ocean fish and the protection of their environment.

National Wildlife Federation
8925 Leesburg Pike
Vienna, VA 22184-0001
(703) 790-4000
Website: http://www.nwf.org
One of the world's largest conservation organizations, this group's mission is to educate, inspire, and assist people to conserve wildlife and other natural resources.

Ocean Voice International
P.O. Box 37026
3332 McCarthy Road
Ottawa, Ontario, Canada K1V 0W0
(613) 990-8819
The mission of this organization is to conserve the diversity of marine life, to protect and restore marine ecosystems, and to promote ecologically sustainable harvest of marine resources.

Pacific Whale Foundation
101 North Kihei Road
Kihei, HI 96753
(808) 879-8860
An organization dedicated to saving whales, dolphins, and their ocean habitats through marine research, public education, and marine conservation.

Visit National Marine Sanctuaries

National marine sanctuaries are protected areas around and along the coasts of the United States. They are administered by the National Oceanic and Atmospheric Administration (NOAA) in the U.S. Department of Commerce and are designed to provide the public with information about marine environments as well as protect the organisms native to those regions.

You and your family may wish to plan a vacation to one or more of these important sites. Write or call for more information.

Channel Islands National Marine Sanctuary
113 Harbor Way
Santa Barbara, CA 93109
(805) 966-7107

Cordell Bank National Marine Sanctuary
Fort Mason Building, #201
San Francisco, CA 94123
(415) 556-3509

Flower Garden Banks National Marine Sanctuary
c/o Texas A&M University Sea Grant Program
1716 Briarcrest Drive, Suite 603
Bryan, TX 77802
(409) 847-9296

Gray's Reef National Marine Sanctuary
30 Ocean Science Circle
Savanna, GA 31411
(912) 598-2345

Gulf of the Farallones National Marine Sanctuary
Fort Mason Building, #201
San Francisco, CA 94123
(415) 556-3509

Florida Keys National Marine Sanctuary
P.O. Box 500368
5550 Overseas Highway
Marathon, FL 33050
(305) 743-2437

Monitor National Marine Sanctuary
Building 1519
Fort Eustis, VA 23604-5544
(804) 878-2973

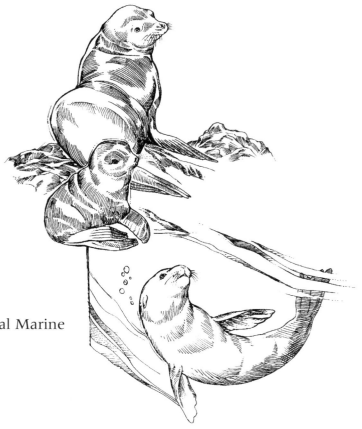

Monterey Bay National Marine Sanctuary
299 Foam Street, Suite D
Monterey, CA 93940
(408) 647-4201

Hawaiian Islands Humpback Whale National Marine
    Sanctuary
726 South Kihei Road
Kihei, HI 96753
(808) 879-2818

Olympic Coast National Marine Sanctuary
138 West First Street
Port Angeles, WA 98362-2600
(360) 457-6622

Stellwagen Bank National Marine Sanctuary
14 Union Street
Plymouth, MA 02360
(508) 747-1691

Read Other Books About the Oceans

The following books can provide you with loads of additional information and fascinating facts about the oceans. In these books you'll discover strange and unusual animals, incredible information about oceans and seas, and wonderful data you'll want to share with your family and friends. Plan to obtain some of these books from your local bookstore, public library, or school library.

Aliki. *My Visit to the Aquarium.* New York: HarperCollins, 1996.
A variety of marine habitats are explored in this well-done introduction to an aquarium.

Anderson, Madelyn. *Oil Spills.* New York: Watts, 1990.
Describes the problem of oil spills, their effect on the environment, and what must be done to clean up after them.

Arnold, Caroline. *Killer Whale.* New York: Morrow, 1994.
Presents the behavior and characteristics of killer whales. An excellent book by an outstanding writer.

———. *Watch Out for Sharks.* New York: Clarion, 1991.
A thorough and complete introduction to the world of sharks. Dispels some myths and provides welcome information about these misunderstood creatures.

———. *A Walk by the Seashore.* Englewood Cliffs, N.J.: Silver Press, 1990.
A young child and an adult take a walk along the seashore and discover some marvelous treasures and surprises.

———. *A Walk on the Great Barrier Reef.* Minneapolis, Minn.: Lerner, 1988.
The many forms of life on Australia's Great Barrier Reef are described in this exciting book.

Arnosky, Jim. *Crinkleroot's 25 Fish Every Child Should Know.* New York: Macmillan, 1993.
An indentification guide to salt- and freshwater fishes.

Bailey, Jill. *The Life Cycle of a Crab.* New York: Bookwright Press, 1990.
Lots of fascinating information about the life cycle of a crab is included in this well-illustrated book.

93

Baines, John. *Protecting the Oceans.* Austin, Tex.: Raintree Steck-Vaughn, 1991.
Describes the importance of and threats to the ocean environment and measures what practices may curb these threats.

Baker, Lucy. *Life in the Oceans.* New York: Watts, 1990.
Presents readers with a thorough overview of ocean life and some of its most interesting elements.

Bellamy, David. *Our Changing World: The Rock Pool.* New York: Crown, 1988.
This book tells the story of cleaning up a rock pool in the aftermath of an oil spill and describes the return of life to the area.

Bendick, Jeanne. *Exploring an Ocean Tide Pool.* New York: Holt, 1994.
Examines the ecosystem of a tide pool. Discusses tides, tidal zones, and the plants and animals found in a tide pool.

Bright, Michael. *Humpback Whale.* New York: Gloucester Press, 1990.
Maps, photographs, and lots of fantastic information are highlighted in this book about a magnificent creature.

Carr, Terry. *Spill! The Story of the Exxon Valdez.* New York: Watts, 1991.
This book introduces the 1989 Alaskan oil spill and its effects on the wildlife, ecosystem, and economy.

Coldrey, Jennifer. *Life in the Sea.* New York: Bookwright Press, 1990.
Wonderful photography and lots of clearly presented information highlight this all-inclusive book.

Cole, Joanna. *The Magic School Bus on the Ocean Floor.* New York: Scholastic, 1994.
Miss Frizzle and her class take a marvelous journey through the ocean's depths to learn some important information.

Corrigan, Patricia. *Dolphins for Kids.* Minocqua, Wisc.: NorthWord, 1996.
A young girl discovers some fascinating and interesting information about the lives of dolphins. Great photography and delightful illustrations highlight this book.

Davidson, Margaret, and Sharon Bakoske. *Dolphins!* New York: Random House, 1993.
A very basic introduction to the life of dolphins.

Doubilet, Anne. *Under the Sea from A to Z.* New York: Crown, 1991.
An alphabet book that describes unusual sea plants and animals.

Fowler, Allan. *It Could Still Be a Fish.* Chicago: Children's Press, 1990.
A great introduction to the world of fish for very young readers. Lots of
   super photographs.

Ganeri, Anita. *I Wonder Why the Sea Is Salty and Other Questions About the
   Ocean.* New York: Kingfisher, 1995.
This book answers questions about the ocean, marine ecology, and ma-
   rine life.

————. *The Oceans Atlas.* New York: Dorling Kindersley, 1995.
Packed full of information about major aspects of ocean life, this book is
   a "must-have" for any serious oceanographer.

Gibbons, Gail. *Whales.* New York: Holiday House, 1991.
Lots of detailed information highlight this text about some of the most
   majestic creatures in the oceans. A highly recommended book.

Greenaway, Frank. *Tide Pool.* New York: Dorling Kindersley, 1992.
Discusses the different kinds of plants and animals that can be found in
   tide pools and how they interact with one another.

Greenway, Shirley. *Animal Homes: Water.* Brookfield, Conn.: Newington
   Press, 1991.
An appealing introduction to the wide variety of life that inhabits the
   world's oceans.

Hirschi, Ron. *Where Are My Puffins, Whales, and Seals?* New York: Bantam, 1992.
This book describes the multitude of life found in and around the sea
   and how that life is being endangered by marine pollution.

————. *Ocean.* New York: Bantam, 1990.
Colored drawings and high-quality photos compliment this description
   of a varity of ocean creatures.

Hoff, Mary, and Mary Rodgers. *Our Endangered Planet: Oceans.* Minneapolis, Minn.: Lerner, 1991.
Describes the threats posed by our use of the world's oceans.

Hogan, Paula. *Dying Oceans.* Milwaukee, Wisc.: Gareth Stevens, 1991.
A basic introduction to the reasons why many oceans around the world
   are endangered.

Johnson, Sylvia. *Hermit Crabs.* Minneapolis, Minn.: Lerner, 1989.
An informative, well-written introduction to the unusual behaviors of
   the hermit crab.

————. *Crabs*. Minneapolis, Minn.: Lerner, 1982.
An introduction to the life cycle and physical characteristics of crabs.

Kagen, Neil, ed. *Do Fish Drink? First Questions and Answers About Water.* New York: Time-Life, 1993.
Lots of questions and lots of answers about oceans and their inhabitants are featured in this book.

Kite, Patricia. Do*wn in the Sea: The Crab*. Morton Grove, Ill.: Whitman, 1994.
Attractive and easy to read with many fascinating facts about the life of crabs.

————. *Down in the Sea: The Jellyfish*. Morton Grove, Ill.: Whitman, 1993.
Easily understood, this book has lots of spendid photographs throughout.

————. *Down in the Sea: The Octopus*. Morton Grove, Ill.: Whitman, 1993.
An attractive and readable introduction to the octopus.

Lazier, Christine. *Seashore Life*. Ossining, N.Y.: Young Discovery Library, 1991.
Lots and lots of factual information about the enormous variety of life at the seashore.

Ling, Mary. *Amazing Fish*. New York: Knopf, 1991.
Examines the behavior and habitats of a wide variety of ocean fish.

Love, John. *Sea Otters*. Golden, Colo.: Fulcrum Publishing, 1992.
The habitat, behavior, and history of sea otters is presented with appealing illustrations by the author.

Macquitty, Miranda. *Ocean*. New York: Knopf, 1995.
Incredible photographs and loads of fascinating information distinguish this book as one of the finest on ocean life.

Maddern, Eric. *Curious Clownfish*. Boston: Little, Brown, 1990.
A wonderfully illustrated story about a young fish who sets out to see the world.

Maestro, Betsy. *A Sea Full of Sharks*. New York: Scholastic, 1990.
Everything you would ever want to know about sharks is in this informative and highly entertaining book.

Malnig, Anita. *Where the Waves Break: Life at the Edge of the Sea*. Minneapolis, Minn.: Lerner, 1987.
Beautiful photographs help introduce the young reader to life at the seashore.

Martin, James. *Tentacles: The Amazing World of Octopuses, Squid, and Their Relatives*. New York: Crown, 1993.
A lively and scientific introduction to these wonderful, and often misunderstood, sea creatures.

May, John. *The Greenpeace Book of Dolphins*. New York: Sterling, 1990.
An invaluable resource and wonderful introduction to the world of dolphins.

McDonald, Megan. *Is This a House for a Hermit Crab?* New York: Orchard Books, 1990.
A hermit crab seeks shelter in this wonderful story enhanced with delightful and engaging illustrations.

McGovern, Ann. *The Desert Beneath the Waves*. New York: Scholastic, 1991.
This wonderful book describes some of the unusual sea creatures that live on the ocean bottom.

McMillan, Bruce. *Going on a Whale Watch*. New York: Scholastic, 1992.
Two 6 year olds on a whale-watching expedition see different types of whales. Includes lots of factual information.

McNulty, Faith. *Listening to Whales Sing*. New York: Scholastic, 1996.
A young girl tries to understand the song of a whale in this story, which teaches about environmental preservation and endangered species.

Miller, Christina and Louise Berry. *Coastal Rescue: Preserving Our Seashores*. New York: Atheneum, 1989.
Examines different types of coasts, how they are shaped by nature, and ways to use the coast's valuable resources.

Oppenheim, Joanne. *Oceanarium*. New York: Bantam, 1994.
This book takes an imaginative approach to tidal waters and the deep sea.

Pallotta, Jerry. *The Underwater Alphabet Book*. Watertown, Mass.: Charlesbridge Publishers, 1991.
This book is an alphabetic journey describing common and unusual creatures that inhabit the world's oceans.

Parker, Steve. *Fish*. New York: Knopf, 1990.
Lots of photos and an engaging text highlight some amazing sea creatures.

———. *Seashore*. New York: Knopf, 1989.
Introduces the various animals and plants of the seashore and discusses the importance of preservation.

Penny, Malcolm. *Let's Look at Sharks.* New York: Bookwright Press, 1990. Provides the reader with basic information about some of the world's most well-known sharks, their habits and habitats.

Pratt, Kristen. *A Swim Through the Sea.* Nevada City, Calif.: Dawn Publications, 1994.
This richly illustrated book uses the letters of the alphabet to introduce a wide variety of ocean life.

Rinard, Judith. *Along a Rocky Shore.* Washington, D.C.: National Geographic, 1990.
Clear and crisp photographs introduce the reader to life along a rocky shore.

Shale, David. *World of a Jellyfish.* Milwaukee, Wisc.: Gareth Stevens, 1987.
Everything the young scientist would want to know about these amazing creatures.

Silver, Donald. *One Small Square: Seashore.* New York: Freeman, 1993.
A wonderful book for the budding oceanographer. Lots of projects and activities throughout this magnificently illustrated book. A definite "must-have."

Simon, Seymour. *Oceans.* New York: Morrow, 1990.
With rich photographs this book provides numerous insights into the major features of the world's oceans.

————. *Whales.* New York: HarperCollins, 1990.
A rich introduction to the behavior, habits, and habitats of whales. Complete with photographs.

Snedden, Robert. *What Is a Fish?* San Francisco: Sierra Club Books for Children, 1993.
This book answers the questions kids ask most about fish such as how gills work, how fish hear, and how some fish communicate.

Souza, Dorothy. *Powerful Waves.* Minneapolis, Minn.: Carolrhoda Books, 1992.
This books focuses on the power of tsunamis (tidal waves).

Steele, Philip. *Killers: Fish.* Englewood Cliffs, N.J.: Julian Messner, 1991.
A highly interesting book about why animals kill and are killed. A good introduction to the concept of predator and prey.

Swanson, Diane. *Safari Beneath the Sea.* San Francisco: Sierra Club Books for Children, 1994.
An outstanding presentation with fascinating descriptions of both familiar and unusual aspects of sea life.

Turbak, Gary. *Ocean Animals in Danger.* Flagstaff, Ariz.: Northland Publishing, 1994.
Introduces about a dozen endangered marine animals.

Wells, Susan. *The Illustrated World of Oceans.* New York: Simon and Schuster, 1993.
An atlas of the earth's oceans with illustrations and information about their history, inhabitants, exploration, and uses.

Wexo, John. *Whales.* Mankato, Minn.: Creative Education, 1990.
A magnificent overview of the whales of the world. A highly recommended book for older readers.

Wheeler, Alwyne. *Discovering Saltwater Fish.* New York: Watts, 1988.
A guide to some of the more easily recognizable fish in the ocean.

Williams, Brian. *Under the Sea.* New York: Random House, 1989.
An illustrated introduction to the world under the sea and the special diving machines that probe the ocean depths.

Wu, Norbert. *Fish Faces.* New York: Holt, 1993.
The author, a marine biologist and underwater photographer, uses magnificent color photos to introduce a variety of fishes and their characteristics.

———. *Beneath the Waves: Exploring the Hidden World of the Kelp Forest.* San Francisco: Chronicle Books, 1992.
A day in the kelp forest introduces a variety of marine life. Highlighted with excellent photos.

———. *Life in the Oceans.* New York: Bookwright Press, 1990.
Spectacular photographs and lots of interesting information offers the reader a glimpse into selected aspects of ocean life.

Websites

The following websites can provide you with valuable background information and up-to-the-minute research about the oceans of the world. Take a look at aquariums around the world, find out some of the fascinating work being done on the ocean floor, get a glimpse into the mysterious world of deep-sea creatures, and take a ride on all sorts of oceanic research vessels. There is much to learn and much to explore on these websites.

Note: These websites were current and accurate as of the writing of this book. Please be aware that some may change, others may be eliminated, and new ones will be added to the various search engines that you use at home or at school.

http://vpm.com/cordova/

This is a super website developed by teachers and students at an elementary school in California. Lessons on squids, sharks, fish, coastal ecosystems, and lots of other ocean activities are included.

http://www.turtles.org/

This is a great website that focuses on marine turtles, where they live, why they are endangered, and what we can do to save them.

http://www.aboveall.com/bb/BBMAIN.html

Here's a great website that has dozens of photographs of ocean reefs and reef animals from around the world.

http://seaweed.ucg.ie/Seaweed.html

Everything you would ever want to know about seaweed can be found here—cultivation, food, databases, links, pictures, and uses are just some of the links.

http://www.actwin.com/fish/species.cgi

At this site you can see more than 200 photographs of various marine organisms from around the world.

http://www.oceans.net/preserve.html

This website offers information on the preservation and protection of oceans as well as an index of resources.

http://inspire.ospi.wednet.edu:8001/curric/oceans/

This site offers instructional units and projects on a variety of topics—tracking drifter buoys, investigating ocean currents, ocean color, and plant life in the ocean.

http://www.oceans.net/

The ultimate source for scuba diving in the ocean.

http://www.nos.noaa.gov/

The National Ocean Service is the primary agency responsible for the health and safety of our nation's oceans. Find out about their services and products on this website.

http://www.pbs.org/kratts/world/oceans/index.html

This website provides up-to-the-minute information about oceans and ocean creatures from around the world.

http://seawifs.gsfc.nasa.gov/OCEAN_PLANET/HTML/resource_data_services.html

This website is a listing of oceanography-related resources that can be found on the Internet. Exploration of these resources will turn up a surprising variety of information.

10 Fantastic Facts

... About Fish and Other Creatures

A shrimp's heart is in its head.

An octopus has three hearts.

The male seahorse carries around the eggs until they hatch.

Krill, a shrimplike creature that lives in polar waters, jumps out of its shell when scared.

Parrotfish secrete a jellylike bubble around their bodies for protection while sleeping.

Sponges are animals.

Starfish have no brains.

The largest recorded squid was found in 1878. It weighed 2 tons and was about 50 feet long. Each of its eyes was more than 15 inches across.

The biggest fish in the world is the whale shark, which can reach a length of 59 feet and a weight of 20 tons.

The giant spider crab, from claw tip to claw tip, measures more than 140 inches.

The sea robin, a tropical fish, has 6 appendages that allow it to "walk" over the ocean bottom. It also makes a sound like a frog.

The world's smallest shark is the dwarf shark, which reaches a total length of only 6 inches.

The giant clam of the South Pacific can grow up to 4 feet across and weigh more than 500 pounds.

Walking catfish in Florida can stay out of the water for as long as 80 days.

When lobsters can't find anything to eat, they eat each other.

... About Marine Mammals

A full-grown female blue whale is 25 times heavier than the world's largest land animal, the male African elephant.

Baby blue whales can weigh up to 5 tons at birth and drink as much as 130 gallons of milk a day.

Gray whales make an annual migration of more than 12,500 miles from the Arctic Ocean to southern Mexico and back.

Sperm whales can hold their breath for almost 2 hours while they dive for food.

The tongue of a grown blue whale weighs more than most elephants.

The sperm whale's brain weighs more than 20 pounds. (A human brain only weighs 3 pounds.)

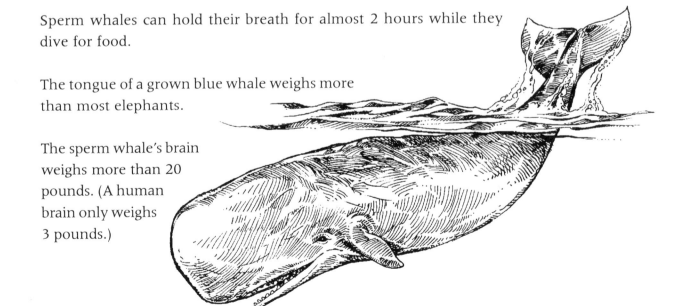

... About Ocean Plants

Seaweed is the fastest growing plant in the world.

The Pacific giant kelp can grow to a length of more than 190 feet. Amazingly, this plant can grow 18 inches a day.

The first ocean plants were blue-green algae, which first appeared more than 3.5 billion years ago.

The algae of the world's oceans produce nearly 50 percent of the world's oxygen.

giant kelp

... About Strange Critters

A bootlace worm found in the North Sea measured more than 178 feet in length.

Barnacles carry their ovaries in their heads.

Octopi have 1 little eye to see things in sunlit waters and 1 big eye to see things in dark waters.

Oysters can change their sex from male to female to male and so on, throughout their lives.

The box jellyfish's venom can kill a person in 30 seconds.

The horseshoe crab has remained unchanged for more than 300 million years.

The linckia starfish produces babies by dropping off all of its legs, which in turn grow into new starfish.

The black torpedo ray generates enough electricity to power a television set.

The candlefish is so rich in oils that it can be dried, fitted with a wick, and burned like a candle.

95 percent of a jellyfish is water.

horseshoe crab

... About Predators and Prey

Starfish eat their prey by pushing their stomachs outside their bodies and secreting digestive juices directly on their victims.

The great white shark can detect 1 part of blood in 100 million parts of water.

The Portuguese man-of-war, a type of jellyfish, grows tentacles that are 100 feet long.

A meat-eating shark has up to 3,000 teeth in its mouth.

A sea cucumber protects itself by ejecting its stomach over an approaching enemy. It can regrow its guts in a few weeks.

The poison of a blue-ringed octopus is more deadly than that of any land animal.

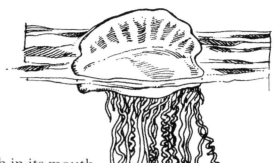

Portuguese man-o-war

... About Oceans Near and Far

About 30 percent of the world's salt supply comes from the oceans.

Huge storm waves hitting shore can pick up rocks from the ocean floor that weigh as much as 7,000 pounds and throw them on land.

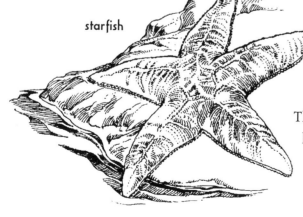

starfish

If a 2-pound steel ball was dropped into the Marianas Trench, it would take over 1 hour to reach the bottom.

Ocean waves sometimes go as far as 1,000 feet below the ocean's surface.

The highest recorded natural wave was 112 feet high.

The Mediterranean Sea is the world's most polluted sea. More than 421 billion tons of pollution are poured into it every year.

The saltiest sea water is found in the Red Sea.

The oceans of the world cover an area that is 37 times the size of the United States.

The sea level is rising by about 3 inches every 100 years.

The United States has a shoreline of more than 88,000 miles.

Waves can travel as far as 2,000 miles across the ocean without losing any energy.

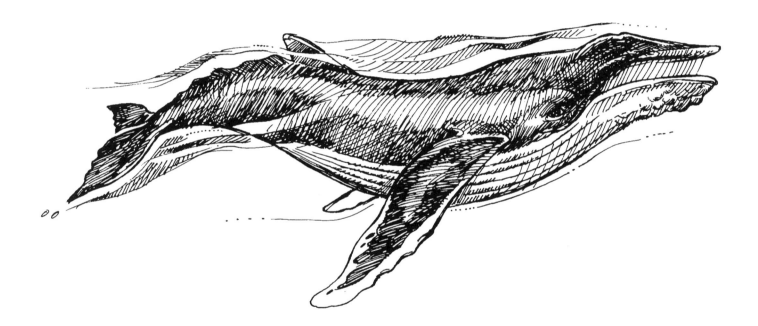

Glossary

Abyss: The great depths of the ocean floor—usually with depths of 15,000 feet or more.

Abyssal plain: A vast, flat, barren area on the sea floor that spreads from the mid-oceanic ridge to where the continents begin.

Antarctic: The extremely cold region at the South Pole, which is south of the Antarctic Circle.

Arctic: The very cold region at the North Pole, which is north of the Arctic Circle.

Basin: A large, cup-shaped dent in the ocean floor.

Bathysphere: A sphere-shaped diving vessel used by scientists to study deep-sea life.

Bay: A part of a larger body of water that cuts into a shoreline, forming a curve.

Beaufort Scale: A scientific scale used to indicate the strength of the wind at sea.

Biodegradable: The ability of a substance or material to break down into harmless substances by the action of living organisms.

Bioluminescence: The production of light by living organisms. Some deep-sea creatures can produce their own, while others rely on the light produced by bacteria that live in or on them.

Black smokers: Mineral chimneys on the ocean floor. They spew black smoke and very hot water rich in sulphur, which some deep sea organisms use to make food.

Breaker: A wave whose crest falls forward and crashes.

Camouflage: The shape or color of an animal that allows it to blend in with its surroundings to hide and avoid predators or to catch food.

Carnivore: An animal that eats other animals or meat for food.

Cetaceans: The group of marine mammals with teeth, including whales, porpoises, and dolphins.

Climate: The type of weather that is normally expected in an area of the world over a long period of time (years, for example). In general, we expect the tropics' climate to be hot and wet and the arctic's climate to be very cold.

Continental drift: The theory that all the earth's landmasses were once one single body of land that separated over many millions of years forming what we now know as the continents.

Continental shelf: A flat, projecting extension of land submerged beneath a shallow sea.

Continental slope: The gently sloping, submerged land near the coastline that forms the side of an ocean basin.

Crest: The top of a wave.

Crustacean: An animal, such as a lobster or crab, that has a hard skeleton on the outside of its body.

Current: A body of water that flows through the sea.

Diatom: A single-celled plant that often floats near the surface of the ocean. It usually is the first organism in a food chain or food web.

Dorsal fin: A fin on the back of a fish. It helps a fish keep its balance as it moves through the water.

Ecology: The study of the relationship between plants and animals (including humans) and their environment.

Ecosystem: All the living organisms and the physical features within a specific area.

Environment: Our surroundings—including all the living and nonliving elements.

Evaporation: The process whereby a liquid, such as water, changes into a vapor or gas.

Food chain: A series of plants and animals linked by their feeding relationships.

Food web: A series of several food chains, which overlap and interconnect.

Gill: The organ that many sea creatures use for breathing.

Guyot: An underwater volcano with a flat top.

Habitat: The place where an animal lives.

Herbivore: An animal that eats plants or plant life.

Iceberg: A large floating chunk of ice, broken off from a glacier and carried out to sea on ocean currents.

Interdependence: The idea that everything in nature is connected to everything else; what happens to one plant or animal also affects other plants and animals.

Invertebrate: An animal without a backbone.

Kelp: Any one of a large variety of brown seaweeds.

Krill: A shrimplike creature that lives in large numbers in polar waters.

Marine biology: The study of ocean life.

Marine park: An area of the ocean set aside as a reserve to protect endangered species and to preserve the marine environment.

Mollusk: An animal, such as a snail, squid, or octopus, with no backbone and a soft body that can be enclosed or partially enclosed by a shell.

Nautical mile: A mile as measured at sea—equal to 6,076 feet (a land mile is equal to 5,280 feet).

Navigation: The science of directing the course of travel for a ship.

Neap tide: The smallest rise and fall in tides that occurs when the sun and the moon are at right angles to the earth.

Nutrients: Substances necessary for the life and growth of living organisms.

Oceanic ridge: A long, narrow chain of underwater mountains formed when two of the earth's plates meet and magma wells up to the surface to form a new sea floor.

Oceanic trench: A long, narrow valley under the sea that contains some of the deepest points on earth.

Oceanographer: A scientist who studies the ocean, its topography, and its inhabitants.

Oceanography: The science of studying the ocean.

Plankton: Tiny plant or animal organisms that drift near the surface of the water and which form an important link in the food chain.

Pollutant: A substance that destroys the purity of air, water, or land.

Predator: An animal that preys on other animals for food.

Raw sewage: Untreated liquid waste from drains, toilets, and sewers.

Runoff: The part of precipitation that washes from the land into bodies of water, such as the ocean.

Sea breeze: A movement of cool air from the ocean to the land.

Seamount: An underwater mountain.

Sediment: Mineral or organic matter that contains millions of tiny animals and plants and which settles on the bottom of the sea.

Spring tide: The greatest rise and fall in tides that occurs when the sun and the moon are in line with the earth.

Submersible: A small submarine that is able to reach the depths of the ocean or that is able to probe inside places that are too small for ordinary vessels.

Surface layer: The top layer of seawater—the layer with the warmest water and where the temperature changes only slightly with depth.

Tentacle: A slender flexible feeler that enables an animal with no backbone to touch things.

Tide: The repeating rise and fall of the earth's sea, caused by the pull of the moon and sun on the water.

Tide pool: An area along the rocky coast that is covered by water during part of the day and exposed to the air during the other part of the day.

Trench: A deep gash or valley in the ocean floor.

Tropical storm: A spinning storm in the tropics with wind speeds of 39 to 73 mph.

Trough: The lowest point in a wave between crests.

Tsunami: A gigantic, often destructive wave, which is usually triggered by an undersea volcano or earthquake. Also referred to as a tidal wave.

Typhoon: A hurricane in the western Pacific Ocean.

Wave height: The horizontal distance between the crest and trough of a wave. This distance is measured from the back of the wave.

Wavelength: The distance between 2 successive crests.

Weather: The atmospheric conditions that happen in an area during a specific and short period of time, such as a few hours or a few days.

Zooplankton: Small animals that drift in the ocean.

Index

About the Author

Anthony D. Fredericks has written more than 30 teacher resource books in the areas of science, social studies, and language arts, including *Exploring the Rainforest* (Fulcrum, 1996) and *From Butterflies to Thunderbolts*, (Fulcrum, 1997) as well as children's books on animals, nature, and environmental studies. He teaches elementary methods courses in science and language arts at York College in York, Pennsylvania.